EDITORS

Diane West, editor

Patsy Dale, chief sub-editor, Macmillan Open Learning

Judy McBride, sub-editor

PROJECT MANAGEMENT

Eimer Rogers, Macmillan Open Learning

CRITICAL READERS

Dot Balgarnie, formerly nurse teacher, North Yorkshire College of Health

Maggie Cotter, administration manager, Macmillan Open Learning

Richard Freeman, training materials consultant

Linda Husband, lecturer, Humberside College of Health

Kevin Thornton, operational manager, Open Learning Programmes,
Lancashire College of Nursing and Health Studies

STUDENT TESTERS

Siobhan Crossan

Carol Edge

Caroline Ford

Dave Tomlin

For my mother and Sophie Louise

STUDY SKILLS FOR ADULT LEARNERS

KAREN RAWLINS

With contributions from
Cathy Hull, Head of Curriculum Development and Publishing, Macmillan
Open Learning, and **Imrana Ghumra,** BA(Hons), Information and Library
Studies Centre Librarian, Humberside College of Health, Scunthorpe

First edition 1996

Published by
Macmillan Magazines Ltd
Porters South
Crinan Street
London N1 9XW

Companies and representatives throughout the world

Printed by
Barwell Colour Print Ltd
Midsomer Norton
Bath

ISBN 0-333-671813

Contents

Introduction

You may be interested in this book because you are returning to study after a substantial break and feel that there are skills you need to acquire or develop in order to tackle whatever course you are embarking on. Perhaps you have been studying recently and have identified areas in which you would like to improve your study skills. Even if you have not studied for a long time, you will have gained many appropriate skills through your work – paid or voluntary – as well as through your social and domestic life. Although these skills may need to be adapted or developed, learning how to study effectively is as much about understanding yourself as a learner as it is about making any new discoveries about learning itself.

Our approach, therefore, is to introduce you to study by building upon what you already know and can do. This means that you can develop those skills you already have and explore new areas rather than having to relearn existing skills. We will help you to identify which study skills you already possess and which you need to develop. You will also discover how you prefer to learn and how you can get the most out of what you are learning.

Here are a few examples of how adult learners have felt about returning to study:

> 'Education is not for me; it's for clever people.'
> 'I like doing practical things. I don't like reading.'
> 'I've not written an essay for years. I don't know where to start.'
> 'I just wish I felt more confident.'

Our aim is to help you to overcome fears of this kind, build your confidence and develop your skills. In this way you should be able to enjoy what you are learning and become competent at it, which will further boost your confidence.

This book will be particularly useful if the prospect of writing an essay or reading an academic text seems daunting to you. Each chapter has been designed to give you a thorough understanding of the basic skills you need in order to complete your studies effectively. You can use the book in whatever way suits you best. You might, for instance, choose to read it from cover to cover initially, and then select specific topics to return to and explore more thoroughly. Alternatively, you may want to use it to help you with a particular study skill problem you currently face, in which case you can dip into the book and select the appropriate section as you feel the need.

Building confidence is often a key element in making the most of the skills you possess, so in Chapter 1 we focus on this. We look at some of the skills you are likely to need and help you to identify the skills you already have. As people returning to study generally have preconceived ideas about education and their own ability to learn, we examine some of the most common myths.

In Chapter 2, which is called 'Understanding yourself as a learner', you will begin to find out more about what makes you 'tick' as a learner. We explore how the various factors that are unique to you and your particular circumstances can affect your learning. You will be introduced to theories about how adults learn and have the opportunity to identify your preferred learning styles.

Chapter 3 will help you to formulate personal learning goals to keep you focused throughout your course. You are asked to develop a realistic study plan so that you can fit your learning into your daily schedule. Reviewing and evaluating your learning are also important. They will enable you to identify your strengths as well as the areas you need to develop. Keeping a reflective diary or learning journal is a particularly effective part of this process. In this chapter, therefore, we explore the importance of critical reflection and the use of diaries and journals as part of the learning process.

In Chapter 4 we look at the range of resources available to you as a learner. As adult learners, most of us undertake at least some of our study at home. We begin, therefore, by looking at how you can create an appropriate environment in which to study. We then explore how you can use support effectively, both from your tutor and from other people. You will also find advice on how to use libraries and a section about making the most of other learning methods that may be available to you, such as lectures, seminars and group tutorials.

In Chapter 5 we concentrate on how you can develop your reading skills. We begin by looking at the materials which are available and how you might approach your reading. Selecting your reading material is particularly important in enabling you to make the most effective use of your time, so you will find practical advice and suggestions, including a book preview checklist which you can use to evaluate the approach and contents of a text.

Listening is also a crucial study skill and towards the end of this chapter we look at how to listen to lectures, audio-tapes and so on, as well as listening to and learning from peers, tutors and others.

The emphasis of Chapter 6 is on making the notes you take effective in your learning. In it we explore the purposes of note-taking and how to overcome some of the common problems. We discuss different methods of taking notes and how to adapt these to various situations, such as in lectures or when working from written texts. The importance of reviewing your notes and storing them appropriately is also stressed.

The subject of the final chapter is writing essays. We take you through the entire process of writing an essay, from choosing the topic and defining the question through to writing and reviewing your work. In order to make the best use of this chapter you should work on an essay as you tackle it, although you may prefer to read the chapter through first, whether or not you have an essay to work on.

We hope you find this book useful in developing your skills and becoming more confident in your ability to study.

Cathy Hull

A NOTE ON TERMINOLOGY

This book is designed for adult learners, whatever their experience of learning and whatever their subject. Although some of the examples given apply specifically to the field of health care, they can be readily adapted to any situation and subject.

Throughout this text the term 'open learning' has been used because the focus is on independent learning and an active approach to studying. This philosophy is based on the belief that adults learn best when they are self-directed and their learning is related to, and arises from, their experience of work and life in general.

1. Debunking the myths

What skills do you need?

It is likely that you are reading this book because you do not feel that you have all the skills you will need for whatever course of study you are about to start or have recently started. It may be that you are not sure what these skills are, or that you are out of the habit of reading academic material, writing essays and so on.

However, you already have a number of skills gained from your schooling or previous study, and you will develop others as part of the process of doing whatever course you are embarking on. Even if you have not undertaken formal study for some time, it is likely that in your personal and professional activities you have been developing many of the skills required. An extremely important skill, for instance, is the ability to manage your time effectively. If you consider how many responsibilities you currently have, both within and outside work, you will appreciate how effective you already are in establishing your priorities and organising your time. Study skills are, really, life skills. Just as your life experiences contribute to your study skills, many, if not all, of the skills you develop through studying will be useful to you in your work and life generally.

ACTIVITY 1
Make a list of the skills which you think you will need in your current studies.

Now go through your list and consider each skill in turn in relation to the following questions:

- **What experiences have you had which have called for this skill?**
- **How successful have you been in these circumstances?**
- **How important do you feel this skill will be in your course?**
- **Are you confident about this skill or do you need to improve it?**
- **How will you go about improving any weak areas?**

Figure 1 shows some of the types of skills you might have come up with.

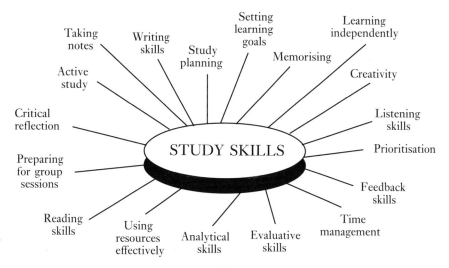

Figure 1. Study skills

As you may have found with your own list, you can see that many of the skills in Figure 1 interrelate, for example, listening and memorising, or prioritisation and time management. The degree of importance each has for you will depend on your previous experience and what stage you have reached in your studies.

You may have come up with skills that are not shown in Figure 1, for example, preparing for examinations. In this book we support the growing movement towards assessment by other means, such as portfolio and continuous evaluation, and so will not discuss this particular skill. However, the chapters on taking notes and writing essays will be useful in any examination preparation you have to undertake.

Some of the skills shown in Figure 1 – taking notes, reading, writing and using resources effectively – are the main subjects of chapters in this book. Others, such as time management, evaluative skills and prioritisation, are discussed as specific topics within chapters. The remaining skills – memorising, creativity and learning independently, for example – are included throughout the book as a whole rather than as specific topics. Taking care of yourself in terms of your sleep patterns, diet and work schedule, for instance, which is discussed in Chapter 2, is crucial to your creativity and your ability to memorise, and is an important aspect of your independent learning.

Whatever kind of course you are starting now, if your previous experience of education was based on being told what, where, when and how to learn, you may need to concentrate on developing your ability to learn independently and to make decisions about your own learning. Even if you have some experience with this, it is probable that there are areas that you could improve, particularly if you are studying at a higher level than previously.

Becoming an independent learner is, for most people, a gradual process and something that you will develop as your confidence in your abilities, experiences and opinions grows.

A valuable first step to any learning is to acknowledge your feelings. This is so that you are not battling against them but, rather, can engage them in helping you move forward in whatever you want to do.

How are you feeling?

How do you feel about your studies? You may feel excited, eager to learn and confident in your abilities; you may also have some niggling self-doubts or anxieties.

ACTIVITY 2
Take a moment to consider your feelings and perhaps make a note of them. What do you notice?

Starting any new course, whatever the level and regardless of any previous achievements or experience of studying, tends to bring with it a mixture of emotions. It is possible that you fluctuate from moments of optimism and enthusiasm to others which are full of doubt and apprehension. These feelings are completely natural and are healthy signs that you want to do your best and that you are gearing yourself up for the demands that lie ahead.

Some feelings, however, could gradually erode your self-confidence if you do not face up to them. If, for instance, you lack confidence in your own abilities, you may find that you talk yourself into failing, thereby confirming your worst suspicions and exacerbating the problem even further. So it is very important that you reflect carefully on your feelings about your studies, not just at the beginning but throughout the course, and that you consider the impact they are having on your approach and general performance.

If you are feeling negative about what you are doing, it is important that you do something about it straight away. This may mean having a chat with your tutor or with fellow students, colleagues, friends or your partner. It doesn't really matter whom you choose. The important thing is to try not to let these feelings build up and fester. Talking about them will help to put them into perspective, especially if you focus on ways to overcome them rather than worrying about how big the problems are.

Positive self-talk

A very useful method for tackling self-doubt, and one that is increasingly used by sports coaches and training consultants, is 'positive self-talk'. This can be an extremely effective way of dealing with problems of any type, including lack of confidence and nerves. It can empower you to overcome any problems with learning that you may have and can be employed in any situation, at any time. Positive self-talk is just that. It involves you imagining success, beginning with a large picture and then examining it in more detail.

If we apply this to a football team which has been underperforming, the goal scorers, for example, might be asked to picture themselves scoring a variety of goals. These could be from a number of positions and from passes by different team members. They would be asked to experience the feelings they might have before, during and after the goal, to picture the noise and reactions from the supporters, their team-mates, coaches and manager, and to try to evoke as much as they can about the atmosphere surrounding the event. When the players have tasted success in their imaginations, they would then be asked to home in on the techniques employed in scoring the goal by concentrating their minds on the position they placed themselves in and how the goal had been scored.

The theory behind such a technique is that if you can see yourself succeeding you will begin to create a positive self-image. By adding more detail to the picture you can then begin to see what it is necessary to do in order to achieve the outcome you want. This can apply equally to overcoming a problem or to a dilemma about how to behave in a certain situation.

The power of self-talk, negative or positive, is immense. We see it every day and you may be able to think of times you have seen it working on friends, colleagues or even yourself. Another sporting analogy that springs to mind is that of Wimbledon fortnight, in particular those unforgettable matches where a player comes from a position of being a number of match points down to winning the match. Dogged determination has much to do with it, as well as talent, of course, but without positive self-talk and an inner belief by the players that they will ultimately succeed, neither of these would be enough. Contrast this with those players who seem to be within an inch of winning and then lose it all – you can almost see their self-belief fade away and the negative self-talk beginning to wreak havoc on their performance.

So how does this relate to study skills? Just as with everything you do, how you feel about yourself and your chances of success has a direct impact on your performance, so using positive self-talk is one way of creating a good self-image and dealing with negative feelings.

ACTIVITY 3
You will need to find someone who is roughly the same build as yourself for this Activity.

1 Decide who is A and who is B.
2 A: Raise your right arm (or left if you are left-handed) straight out sideways at shoulder level.
3 B: Using one arm only, apply pressure on A's arm for a few seconds as if you were trying to push A's arm down. A: Try to keep your arm in the same position.
4 Notice what happens.
5 A: Relax your arm. Close your eyes and say to yourself 10 times: 'I am weak'.
6 Now repeat steps 2, 3 and 4 with B applying the same amount of pressure as before.
7 A: Relax your arm. Close your eyes and say to yourself 10 times:'I am strong'.
8 Repeat 2, 3 and 4 again.

You may want to do the whole exercise again, swapping round who is A and who is B.

You are likely to have found that, even in this very simple exercise, self-talk is effective. You can use this to help you with your studies, perhaps by picturing, in as much detail as possible, a scene in which you receive your certificate for successfully completing your course. You could also give yourself an affirmation to repeat, such as: 'I can learn easily', or 'I am good at writing essays', which you write on a piece of card and keep in a prominent place when you are studying; or you could picture yourself, again in as much detail as possible, studying and getting through your work in the way you want to.

Educational myths

The feelings that you identified in Activity 2 are probably typical of most students. Many people believe, however, that their doubts are not shared by other learners studying the same course, or at least not to the same extent. This view can persist for some time, particularly if contact is not established with other students early on in the course. Comparing your own abilities with those of others is a natural response to a new situation, even where there are no direct competitors. Believing that you are somehow inferior to others – those you think of as 'super-students' – can be an attitude you adopt, particularly if you have been out of formal education for some time.

Such a negative viewpoint is not conducive to a successful and enjoyable educational experience and is an example of one of a collection of myths that surround formal study. How many myths you accept as truths will depend to a large extent on your self-image and confidence, and also on your previous experience of studying. Even the most experienced students, however, can find themselves taking certain myths to heart, particularly if the level of the course is higher than anything they have tackled previously. The title of a course in itself can be enough of a catalyst to spark off a whole host of myths, especially a degree course, which can provoke the reaction: 'But I'm not clever enough to do a degree!'.

ACTIVITY 4
Work through the following statements and note down your reactions to each.

It is very important that you are as honest with yourself as possible. It may help if you do this exercise quickly, using your immediate rather than a considered reaction. You may, for ►

instance, find that your brain tells you one thing, but your feelings say something different.

- My own opinion isn't valid when compared with a theory
- If a writer's name is preceded by the title 'Doctor' or 'Professor', the opinions of that person must be right
- There is a special academic style that adds weight to your opinions and suggests you know what you are talking about
- Whatever anyone says, quantity when writing an essay does help to indicate that you have been thorough in your preparation and that you know your subject
- Other students are more clever than I am and more suited to this course than I am
- Other students have access to more facilities and have more time than I have
- There is only one right answer or approach to an essay question
- Sharing my work and ideas with other students will leave me vulnerable to being copied by others; this wouldn't be fair as I have done all the work.

If the course you are undertaking is described as 'open learning' or 'distance learning' you may also have these thoughts:

- Open learning is a second-best option; face-to-face tuition and a more traditional approach would be preferable if only it were practical
- As an open learner I am on my own.

What effects do your reactions to these statements have on you and your ability to learn? How do you think that your reactions and the attitudes they reflect developed?

The above statements reflect beliefs held by adult students from all levels of courses. But such beliefs are simply not true and they can be very destructive in a variety of ways. Students who think they are true almost certainly inhibit their own performance and fail to benefit from everything a formal learning experience has to offer. For distance learners it is particularly important that the myths surrounding educational study are debunked from the start, as without regular face-to-face contact with other students and tutors they can persist for much longer. Some of these attitudes are now examined in order to discover what lies behind them.

1. Is your opinion valid?

Students often believe that their opinion is less valid than that of a supposed authority on the subject such as a professor, author or theorist.

Learners who feel inhibited about expressing their personal viewpoints when writing an essay or reading a text are essentially devaluing their own experiences and opinions in favour of someone else's.

It is important, particularly with the increasing emphasis on critical reflection and the need to relate academic education to professional practice, that you think about what you are presented with and come to your own conclusions about it. If you are not able to relate your existing experiences to what you are learning and critically evaluate this against real life, then how are you going to apply the principles you have learned back in the workplace?

If you think about it, we are all benefiting or suffering from a plethora of theories that affect our everyday lives. Our children are taught according to current educational theory, the economic and political environments in which we live are affected by the theories adopted by politicians, and theories abut nutrition dictate which foods we are advised to eat or avoid. But these theories are continually being challenged and changed, and most of us readily dismiss the theories with which we don't agree and adopt those with which we do.

If in life generally you are able to do this, then you should be able to do it during your studies as well. It may be that you feel less confident about the subject matter and that a more rigorous and objective analysis of a theory is required, but essentially the principles remain the same. That is to say, theories are just that! They are not fact; they are someone's, or a group of people's, opinions, which may later become dated or out of fashion. Many theories are derived from direct observation of the very experiences that you may ignore as irrelevant.

Theories certainly have an important place in a formal learning context as they provide the learner with the opportunity to share the thinking that has arisen from extensive research and direct observation of the topic in question. At their best they offer an interpretation or rationale behind a set of events which can then be applied in a practical context or framework by the learner.

So it is a good idea to consider the theories and opinions of experts seriously, but also to remember that your opinion is valid and worth expressing.

2. Is there such a thing as an academic writing style?

This question is indicative of a general belief held by many learners that there is some kind of mysterious component to studying, particularly at degree level. There can be the conception that degree-level students are not ordinary folk, but super-talented and brainy men and women who know everything about everything.

We will look at what is required for different levels of studying when we discuss writing essays in Chapter 7. Suffice it to say at this point that there is no such thing as a specific writing style required for any particular educational level, including degrees. The key to an effective style at all levels is the use of clear, concise and plain language, whether or not you need to include technical terminology. Short sentences are preferable to the long, rambling variety, which are unwieldy and often serve only to obscure the point you are trying to make.

The desire to sound intellectual can have serious consequences for learners as it may tempt them to use the words of others as their own. Plagiarism, from whatever motive, is always treated very seriously by academic establishments. It is easy to detect when students are not using their own words. Even if this were not the case, you are not really learning if you do not think about, make sense of and, where possible, discuss what you are learning in order to absorb it and make it your own.

Concentrate on developing your own unique style, using your own 'voice', and avoid embellishments and styles that are contrived or pretentious. This will help you to produce essays that flow naturally and to concentrate your efforts on presenting a well-thought-out answer.

3. Is quantity important?

Worrying about how long a piece of writing should be is a major preoccupation of many learners. In an examination, panic can register on the faces of some students when someone asks for more paper; perhaps they do not appreciate that it is quite possible to write pages and pages of pure drivel! Quantity is still seen by many as a measure of how well a question is answered – but this is a kind of 'never mind the quality, feel the width' mentality.

In certain cases there is no doubt that quantity is important. Students undertaking a research project or dissertation, for example, will often be given a minimum as well as a maximum number of words required and, if this is not met, they may well be penalised. In the majority of cases, however, no such requirement exists and it is left to the students themselves to decide how long their work should be.

Where no guidance is given and you have some weeks to prepare an answer, quantity can be an issue. It is very easy to produce essays that are wordier than they should be. The guideline you should bear in mind is that an essay should be as long as it needs to be to say what it needs to say.

A preoccupation with quantity will almost certainly affect the quality of your work; it can lead to waffling which can be seen to indicate that you do not know your subject or how to answer the question. The main things to avoid are:

• Repetition
• Irrelevant information
• Unnecessary information (such as that which can be taken for granted)
• Meaningless embellishments or clichés.

However, you will avoid the pitfalls if you:

• Know your subject
• Prepare appropriately
• Develop a concise writing style.

In a situation where no guidance about length is given, it is quite legitimate to ask your tutor for his or her views. Some may be reluctant to be specific, however, on the grounds that this is part of the learning process or because length should be determined by the individual approach taken by each student.

4. Does the 'super-student' exist?

It is true that, for the vast majority of us, there will be students who are more or less capable than ourselves. Worrying about where you are in relation to others, however, is a waste of energy, can be destructive and will never improve your performance.

Rather than looking at fellow students as competitors, it is a good idea to think of them as potential allies who can provide you with much-needed support, reassurance and practical help, just as you can them. They are ideally placed to understand how you may be feeling, so you should seek out opportunities for networking as soon as possible.

5. Is open learning a second-best option?

Open learning is sometimes seen as being second best to the more traditional modes of education, but this arises out of a misunderstanding about what open learning actually is. For instance, distance and open learning are often thought to be the same, but in reality they are very different.

Open learning is a philosophy of approach, while distance learning describes any type of learning which occurs at a distance, that is, when tutor and student are separated. The reason the two terms are often linked is that open learning is traditionally employed in a distance learning context.

Open learning is learner-centred and, as such, focuses on the needs of the student. This means that learners take control of their own development, including where, what and how they wish to learn. The learning outcomes of an open learning course will therefore tend to be broad, as they depend on the particular needs and wishes of each individual learner.

The type of curriculum used in open learning is generally known as a 'process' curriculum. This provides learning opportunities from which each student will derive his or her own learning needs and outcomes.

In addition, open approaches recognise and value the skills and knowledge already attained by the learner through experiential learning. This is one of the reasons why open learning is so popular with adults.

This type of approach can be contrasted with more traditional and closed philosophies which tend to prescribe the skills and knowledge that are to be learned by the student group as a whole.

Most open learning courses tend to be a combination of both methods. They will offer a degree of direction, including a course syllabus and set assignments. Likewise, traditional courses will often include opportunities for students to participate actively in their learning.

Open learning, therefore, is much more than a practical alternative to face-to-face provision: it is an educational approach in its own right and one that aims to put the learner at the heart of the educational process. It places responsibility for development on the student rather than the tutor and it can be adapted to suit individual needs and paces of learning. This type of approach encourages the development of critical reflection and independent thinking; it recognises that students learn most effectively by relating new knowledge to previous and current experience.

Endnote

This chapter has, it is hoped, helped you to acknowledge and allay any fears and misconceptions that you may have about your studies. Bear in mind that learning is a process of self-development. There is little point in coming to study with all the answers and finding what you are learning easy and non-challenging. Rather, learning is about trying out new ideas, exploring concepts, challenging ourselves and being prepared to say: 'I don't understand. Help!'

We end by reaffirming some of the points made in this chapter:

- Believe in yourself and your ability to succeed. Positive self-talk and the visualisation of the outcome you want is a useful tool in this
- Develop your own writing style and keep it clear, simple and concise
- Concentrate on quality rather than quantity
- Network with other students
- Be aware that the educational process itself brings benefits, including the range of skills you will develop as a result of studying.

2. Understanding yourself as a learner

Beginning a new course of study provides you with a valuable opportunity to reflect on the way you learn. In this chapter you will be exploring yourself as a unique learner and the impact your lifestyle has on the way you learn. Integral to this are your previous experiences of learning and what these reveal about you and your learning preferences. This exploration will help you to make informed choices about the most effective and enjoyable way to study. A crucial tool for the independent learner is a study plan. We will be looking at drawing up study plans in the next chapter. The work in this chapter is an important preparation for that process as you can plan effectively only once you know how, when and where you learn best.

Clarifying your circumstances

People may try to tell you what is, in their opinion, the best approach to learning, but there are many different ways of studying and what works well for one person may not work for another. We are all individuals with a unique set of circumstances and experiences; it is therefore unrealistic to assume that there is one magical formula that leads to success. Even if you have a fair idea of what works for you already, you should give this some thought. Life never stands still and just as there is no one right way for everyone, so there is no one best way for you all the time.

What we are concerned with here is examining some of the personal factors which you need to consider before deciding on the most appropriate approach for you. The way you are right this minute, for example, physically and mentally, will affect the way you are learning now. Factors such as who you are living with, where you are studying, your relationships and your work situation, your values and beliefs and many other influences will determine to a greater or lesser extent how and what you learn.

You need to be aware of these factors and how they influence your ability to learn. Clearly, you will not be able to change everything in your life to facilitate your learning, and we are not advocating that you divert all your energies away from your studies in order to reappraise your personal life. However, simply being more aware of yourself as an individual and your current lifestyle may lead you to make better decisions about your intended approach or to make a few minor changes to help you study.

An example of this is the story of Maria.

Maria's story

Maria decided to return to formal education after some years spent at home raising children. She hadn't really discussed her course with her family and they were unaware of the extent of the demands it placed on her time and energies. Maria was determined that the course wouldn't interfere with her role as a wife and mother, and attempted to carry out all her previous household duties as normal, fitting in her course work as best she could.

It all got just too much and she was on the point of giving up when she had a heart-to-heart with a fellow student who was in similar circumstances. Unlike Maria, Carol had sat down with her family at the outset and made them aware of what she was doing, how important the course was to her and what household responsibilities would have to change as a result. There had been a few initial resentments and the odd dispute, but she had persevered and had enjoyed, on the whole, full backing from her family.

Carol recommended that Maria call a family conference and discuss the situation with them before giving up the course. Maria decided to take Carol's advice and was amazed at the support which followed, with her three children and husband devastated that she had been feeling this way and agreeing to divide up many of the domestic chores so that she had more time to study.

Such a happy ending may not always be possible, but the very process of clarifying your own circumstances should help you to formulate a study approach best suited to your lifestyle and enable you to make minor adjustments wherever possible.

ACTIVITY 1

Think about the factors that would benefit you in your current studies: perhaps having a private study room; support from your colleagues, friends, partner, and family; good health; boundless energy; a strong motivation to succeed; self-belief; feeling happy and contented – anything, in fact, that is likely to have a positive impact on your life. Make a list of what they are for you.

Now think about any factors that may cause you problems or detract from your studies and, again, make a list. You may become tired very easily, for example, or feel that you won't ➤

receive much support from the people around you. Do you feel
pressured into studying and so have little enthusiasm for it? Are
there tensions within your household? How relaxed are you? Are
you worried about your studies?

Look at your two lists and think about how you can make this
knowledge work for you. Are there any changes you can make
immediately which might help? Should you be altering your
intended approach in any way?

You might find it useful to discuss your thoughts following Activity 1 with someone you feel you can talk to. It may be that, in this way, you will be helped to work towards a solution or offered alternative ways of looking at things. Talking over your concerns often helps to keep things in perspective as well as reassuring you that you are not alone in experiencing those kinds of problems.

In doing Activity 1 you may have highlighted a number of basic factors which affect the way you learn. These can easily be overlooked, but they are vital considerations when deciding on your study plan. Some of these factors are examined next.

Physical factors affecting learning

Body rhythms

Many people say that they are 'night owls' while others think of themselves as 'early birds' or 'larks'. This reflects a tendency to be particularly alert at specific times of the day. If you are aware of when you are at your best, you can use this information to plan when to study. Be aware, too, that most of us are less able to concentrate following large meals, so you may decide to choose something less demanding to do after a meal, or alternatively, to designate this time for resting or for some physical activity.

Your body will have many different rhythms throughout each day. Discovering your individual body rhythms, including your need for sleep, exercise, food, social interaction and so on, is important as it will help you to use those periods when you are most alert for activities requiring the greatest degree of concentration.

Food

It is very easy when you are studying to rely on copious cups of coffee or tea, or on sugary snacks such as chocolate to sustain your energy levels. Although this may give you short spells of energy, it will be only temporary and will leave you more tired than before. A well-balanced, nutritious diet will ensure you get the nourishment required to help you concentrate so that you can make the most of your studies. But what does this mean for you?

ACTIVITY 2
Read the following questions and assess whether your current eating habits best serve your needs:

- **Does your diet include all the essential vitamins and minerals?**
- **Do you feel generally well and do you have sufficient energy?**
- **Do you have a number of meals during the day or one big meal?**
- **Do you eat a lot of snacks and, if so, do you find this helpful?**
- **Are you on a diet and, if so, how does this affect your studies?**
- **How do you feel after mealtimes? Do you study straight after a meal?**

Having given some thought to these questions, are there any changes you would like to make to your diet or eating patterns?

If your response to this Activity was that your diet could be improved or that there are times when you are lacking in energy, you may like to consider a change in your eating habits. Having a well-balanced diet is an important aspect of keeping healthy and alert, yet it is so easy, particularly when studying, to acquire bad eating habits. If you are in any doubt about what is a healthy, balanced diet, consult your doctor or a nutritionist.

Sleep

There are no set rules regarding sleep and it is important that you know what is the right amount of sleep for you. Too little sleep will inhibit your ability to sustain your concentration and cope with the more complex areas of your course. Too much sleep, on the other hand, is liable to make you feel sluggish and heady. Being able to recognise the symptoms of when you are not at your best is important, as it will enable you to make decisions as to what and for how long you should study.

Getting to know your own sleep patterns and habits is an important part of your study preparation. A bedtime ritual such as reading before you sleep may help you have a good night, but on the other hand it might prevent you from getting to sleep because your mind is too active. If you feel you are not sleeping as well as you would like, it might be worth trying out different bedtime rituals to find out what works best for you.

Your concentration span is dependent on many different factors such as how you are feeling at the time, how interested you are in the subject, your immediate environment, the extent of any problems you may have, and so on. The ability to assess to what degree you are actively engaging in your learning is very important, as once your interest begins to waiver there will be little to be gained from continuing with what you are doing. The earlier you recognise that you are losing concentration, the easier it will be to do something about it. Common indications are feeling fidgety or uncomfortable, or your mind wandering.

You may have to combine your studies with a number of other responsibilities such as a full-time job, shift work, family commitments, child care, domestic chores or voluntary work. On top of this, you may have a number of other distractions or anxieties to contend with. It is not surprising, therefore, that you may feel tense and anxious at times.

Are you aware of the fact that you are tense at these times? Being able to recognise the symptoms is important as tension can affect your ability to learn.

ACTIVITY 4
How are you feeling at this moment? Are there any areas of your body that are tense?

Think about the times when you are tense – perhaps at particular times of the day or in particular situations. Compare these with times when you are relaxed. What are the different factors? What can you do to reduce the pressure when you become tense or when your concentration is waning?

You may have come up with some ideas that will help you to relieve tension in your particular circumstance or to regain your concentration. Some suggestions are:

- **Take a break from what you are doing**
- **Move on to a different topic, perhaps something less challenging or something in which you have a particular interest**
- **Try relaxation techniques such as yoga, stretching, deep breathing, massage, aromatherapy**
- **Take some gentle exercise to clear your head, for example, going for a walk or a swim, or doing some stretching**
- **Do something self-indulgent, such as taking a long, luxurious bath, or curling up and listening to music**
- **If it is possible that your tension may be caused by eye-strain, have your eyesight checked**
- **Check that the room you are in is well ventilated and that the lighting and heating are conducive to studying**
- **Take a longer break for sport or physical activity.**

Taking a break from studying and work may be the last thing you feel you should do, especially if it is already difficult to fit everything in. However, having another interest, particularly if it includes physical exercise, is not only a normal part of life, but it will also be beneficial to your studies as it will improve your ability to concentrate for longer periods and help you to sleep. Also, taking a break from conscious study allows your subconscious mind time to work on any problems or issues that you have come across. This process can often make a task that seemed difficult much easier when you return to it after a break.

Peter's story

Peter was a very conscientious student and had planned all aspects of his studies in a well laid-out and comprehensive study plan.

As well as doing a physically demanding job as a staff nurse, he was a keen footballer and swimmer. He decided to give up both his sports while he was doing his course as he felt he simply didn't have the time.

Having been so used to doing some sport, however, he found it very difficult to adjust to his new régime and to study for long periods. He also missed the social life he had enjoyed at the local sports club and began to feel cut off from everyone. Despite being exhausted, he also began to find it difficult to get to sleep and consequently would wake up tired.

Because Peter had restricted himself to a régime of work and study, with no opportunities to relax and unwind, he began to feel tense and to suffer headaches and loss of concentration.

He went to a doctor who persuaded him to draw up a more realistic and less punishing schedule with built-in rest or leisure periods. The doctor also encouraged him to try some relaxation techniques. This led Peter to take up yoga, which he found invaluable in helping him unwind and improve his ability to concentrate.

If you are relaxed you will learn more effectively. Exercise is one method of helping to release tensions in your body. Giving up some time from your studies to indulge in a sport or hobby you enjoy isn't something you need to feel guilty about, particularly if you plan your exercise around your study timetable and when it is likely to be most beneficial.

Other people

Your living arrangements can have either a positive or negative effect on your studies. If you are studying mainly at home or you have to juggle your studies with home commitments, working out a satisfactory living pattern with the other people in your house is essential, as seen earlier in the example of Maria.

Gaining the co-operation of others is not always easy and may mean all sides have to make compromises. Studying will inevitably involve a change in your routine and this may take some getting used to by the people who are affected. It is a good idea, therefore, at the start, to seek a commitment from them to these changes. This should help to reduce the risk of future problems, particularly if you make it clear what impact your studying is likely to have.

ACTIVITY 5
Think about the other people in your life – your partner, children, other family, friends, colleagues and so on. Consider the following questions:

- **How will they be affected by your studies and how are they likely to react?**
- **What do you want from them in terms of support or practical help?**
- **Will you receive their support? If not, how can you deal with this?**
- **Have you discussed your studies with them?**
- **How much do they know about your course?**
- **Are they fully aware of the impact that your studies may have on them?**
- **Have you changed your domestic routine in any way to free you to study?**
- **Are you able to allocate sufficient time to your studies?**
- **Have you allocated enough time for your other commitments?**
- **Have you included time with your family and friends?**
- **How can you deal with any pressure you feel related to your home circumstances?**

This list may have raised some issues that you need to deal with in order to make the process of studying as easy as it can be.

Keeping an open dialogue with the people close to you will give them the opportunity to support you and will help you to be aware of how they are feeling.

Your own motivation

People embark on study for a number of different reasons and these can affect their level of motivation and approach to the work.

ACTIVITY 6
Why have you decided to study?

What benefits do you expect from it?

Spend some time on this and write down as many reasons and benefits as you can think of, personal as well as professional.

We learn best when we are clear about what we want out of the learning and in what way it will benefit us. This is particularly important if you don't feel you are studying through personal choice, as your sense of motivation may be limited.

Having a clear set of learning goals can help to keep you focused on what you want from any particular course of study, particularly if you start to lose your motivation. Learning goals are explored in the next chapter.

You may feel tempted to take the quickest and easiest route to completing your course. If you do, however, you will be undervaluing the educational process itself and the many benefits that it can bring you.

For example, learning can:

- Enable you to develop as an independent thinker
- Broaden your horizons and perspective
- Develop your capacity for critical reflection
- Teach or enhance life skills such as writing (including report-writing), time management and problem solving
- Increase your self-confidence and self-esteem
- Boost your career prospects
- Expand your professional knowledge.

Allowing yourself to enjoy your studies, as well as keeping an eye on the outcome and your reasons for starting the course in the first place, are all useful for helping you to stay motivated. Some other things you might like to try are:

- Giving yourself a sense of achievement by keeping a list of topics or areas of study that you can tick off when each one is completed
- Making the learning fun for yourself, perhaps by making aspects of it into a game

- Varying your study activities to keep them interesting
- Rewarding yourself with a treat each time you complete a section of study.

Remember, too, how effective positive self-talk can be, as was discussed in Chapter 1.

Your learning experiences

We have seen in this chapter that in order to understand yourself fully as a learner you need to take into account many things about your current lifestyle and personal circumstances.

These are not, however, the only factors that will affect you. To appreciate fully the type of learner you are requires a much more detailed analysis of your personal experience of learning and how this has contributed to your approach and attitude. This area will not be new to you if you have worked on a personal profile or portfolio, in which case you may choose to skim through the rest of this chapter.

Personal profiling, very simply, is a process in which you review any, or every, aspect of your life to build up a clear picture of yourself. It can be used for the setting of personal goals, the charting of progress and the recording of achievements. It normally includes a review section which helps you to explore your past experiences and how these have influenced your current approaches and attitudes to learning.

If this is a new area for you, or if you feel you can benefit from looking at it again, the rest of this chapter is intended to help you to reflect on your previous learning experiences and to come to some conclusions as to your preferred learning methods. This will enable you to build up a picture of what type of learner you are so that you can make appropriate choices about the best way to learn.

Your learning experiences will not be confined solely to formal education; learning continues in a variety of contexts throughout our lives. Your workplace will most likely be a tremendously important learning environment, and the way in which you embrace the learning opportunities there will tell you a great deal about the way you prefer to learn. You may also have attended evening classes, or learnt to drive or play a musical instrument. All of these are valuable experiences and can help you to understand your relationship with learning.

ACTIVITY 7

Identify three situations which were positive learning experiences for you and where you felt your learning was significant (even if they were not intended as learning).

Describe each experience in a few sentences and consider what it was about each that made it so successful. The following questions might help:

- Why do you think it was such a positive learning experience for you?
- How did you feel about the subject being covered? Was it something you were interested in anyway?
- How challenging was it?
- What role did your teacher/tutor have in the learning process?
- Was your tutor interesting and enjoyable to listen to?
- What influence did his/her approach have on your ability to learn?
- Were there other students and, if so, what effect did they have on you?
- Was there any assessment and, if so, how did you feel about this?
- How much control did you have on how, where and what you learned?
- How much of your learning was directed by others?
- Were there any outside factors that contributed towards how you felt?

Now repeat the exercise for three instances that you feel were negative learning experiences.

Analyse what these recollections tell you about the way you learn. Next, make some notes about how you can apply what you have discovered to your current studies.

Factors influencing learning

You will have come to your own conclusions about the factors that help you and those that hinder you in learning. However, you may have found that one of the ways you learn best is by practical application. When we are told how to do even a fairly simple procedure it may only really make sense to us when we try it out for ourselves. If we have the opportunity to repeat the procedure we will probably quite quickly absorb the learning.

Another important factor in learning is the way it is communicated. An enthusiastic lecturer who gives an entertaining and well-structured talk might leave you feeling positive about a learning event which, if handled by a less skilled lecturer, could have left you feeling quite the reverse.

Your relationship with your teacher is often a crucial factor; so, too, is whether you can make some kind of personal connection with the learning that gives it particular relevance for you. You may not recognise many of your learning experiences as such because they have taken place in the course of everyday life, or you may become aware of them only much later.

Understanding how you learn

Clearly, there are many different factors that influence any learning situation. You may have discovered that you have more than one preferred approach to learning, and you will almost certainly be able to adapt and learn by different methods as the situation dictates, even if they are not ideal for you. However, where you are able make choices as to how you can learn, such as in an open learning context, knowing what type of learner you are can help you to decide the best way to study. For example, if you benefit from mutual learning experiences, you could set up a regular support group with other students or attend a seminar on a particular topic that is causing you difficulties. Knowing how best you learn will also help you decide what you want from your tutor and give you ideas as to how your colleagues and family can help.

Some of the research that has been carried out into how people set about learning can be useful in helping you to understand your own learning style[1].

Surface and deep learners
Surface learners aim to commit information to memory in order to be able to reproduce it as required. They therefore tend to concentrate on the words of the text and on memorising the main facts or large chunks of information. Because they have only a superficial knowledge of the subject, they may have difficulty in applying what they have learned or in attempting a critical analysis of it.

Deep learners, on the other hand, aim to gain a thorough understanding of the subject and hence concentrate on the meaning of what they are learning. They will therefore look beyond the words of the text and try to get at the writer's intentions. Because of this they will be able to give an opinion on what they have read and examine it in the light of their own experiences.

You may find that you tend to use one of these approaches more often than the other, but on the whole most learners will adopt either approach depending on the level and nature of the course they are taking. The danger of the surface approach is that you will not be able to use what you have learned because you don't actually understand it. The usefulness of knowledge without understanding is clearly very limited: you won't be able to apply it either in your professional life or in an essay that demands anything more than straightforward facts. Also, the very process of committing something to memory is made much more difficult if you don't understand it. On the whole, therefore, having a deep understanding of something is more likely to make the subject interesting, memorable and enjoyable, as well as far more useful to you subsequently.

Serialist and holistic learners

Serialist learners divide their subject up and work through each topic, step by step. Their focus tends to be relatively narrow and they will begin a new topic area only when they have a thorough understanding of the first.

Holistic learners prefer to get a feel for the whole subject prior to breaking it down into study components or studying any area in great detail. During this time they may also examine it from different viewpoints or look for connections with what they already know. Such an initial review enables them to gain a broad understanding or overview of the whole picture, including the main themes and general principles that run through each topic.

Both the serialist and holistic learner may be concerned with seeking a deep understanding; it is simply the approach they take that differs. Again, you might feel you tend towards one category more than the other or that you are able to vary your approach according to the situation. If you tend towards being a serialist learner, however, you need to ensure that you gain an understanding of the overall picture so that you can see how the topics relate to each other. Conversely, if you tend to the holistic approach, watch that you don't oversimplify the broad themes or miss drawing important distinctions because you have paid insufficient attention to detail.

Knowing about both strategies can help you to keep your approach flexible enough to benefit from both methods while avoiding the risks inherent in each.

Honey and Mumford's learning styles

The learning theories we have looked at so far offer two opposing approaches. The learning styles theory of Honey and Mumford[2] proposes four types of learner: the activist, the reflector, the theorist and the pragmatist. Of course, learners tend to vary their styles according to the situation and often use more than one style at any one time. With which of the following do you identify most strongly?

1. The activist

Activists are very enthusiastic learners who welcome the challenge that new learning experiences bring. They tend to approach these with huge amounts of energy and enthusiasm and with an open mind. They are very active and particularly enjoy reacting to crises and pressure.

Once the initial excitement is gone, however, they tend to get bored easily and want to move onto something new. As such, they are not good finishers as they get impatient with the finer detail that the implementation and consolidation of learning require.

They are often the extroverts in a group and enjoy being in the limelight.

2. The reflector

Reflectors collect information, both first-hand and by listening to and watching others. They look at things from every angle and consider fully the implications of any action before advocating its implementation. Consequently, they are often able to see things from a number of different perspectives and will think through a problem far more carefully and thoroughly than the activist, who tends to jump in with both feet.

Reflectors are cautious: they try to postpone decision-making for as long as possible and are often the quiet members of the group.

They enjoy watching and listening to others and prefer to take a back seat in discussions and activities.

3. The theorist

Theorists tend to make sense of what they see and experience by putting everything into a theoretical context. They think in a very logical and objective way. Theorists are often perfectionists and will not be content unless every aspect has been placed into an acceptable context or framework. They are happy only to accept things that appear logical and rational.

They are most comfortable dealing with basic assumptions, theories and systems. They tend to look at things clinically and focus on objective argument and rational analysis rather than on anything subjective.

4. The pragmatist

Pragmatists like to try out new ideas and theories to see if they work in practice. They like to get on with things and act confidently and quickly on ideas they like. Pragmatists can become impatient with lengthy debates, particularly if they can't see that these are going to lead to any action. Once they have made up their minds they will want to act straight away.

ACTIVITY 9
What have you discovered about how you learn in a given situation? Give each of the four styles a mark according to how much you feel you identify with them.

Refer back to your responses to Activity 7. How do these experiences relate to what you have discovered about your preferred learning style?

Matching learning styles with learning activities

Some learning activities are strongly geared to one style of learning. If this is also your preferred style, you are in the ideal learning situation. However, this is unlikely to be the case all the time, so an awareness of your preferred learning style can help you to adapt to situations that are not so favourable for you. This may mean avoiding certain activities altogether or getting extra support to tackle them. Generally, however, learners are able to adapt themselves to learning situations which are less than ideal, and often they need to do this.

An awareness of styles can explain particular difficulties you may have come across or clashes with other people who have different approaches. Awareness of your weaknesses as well as your strengths gives you the opportunity to work on them.

Honey and Mumford analysed the types of learning situations which suit each learning style. Below is the type of checklist they produced, which will help you to match your learning activities to your preferred learning style.

The four types of learners and their preferred learning activities

Activists prefer learning environments which:

- Involve lots of different and varied activities
- Challenge and stimulate
- Enable them to take a central role, such as that of group leader
- Encourage risk-taking
- Encourage participants to contribute ideas
- Impose few constraints.

Activists may find it more difficult to learn in situations which require them to be passive, such as listening to a lecture or watching a video. They may react negatively to activities which require them to pay considerable attention to detail or which involve a lot of repetition or reflection. Activists may also become impatient if asked to consider a lot of theoretical information. They generally do not like working in isolation or in situations which constrain them, such as by imposing a very tight structure.

Reflectors prefer learning environments which:

- Encourage reflection and evaluation
- Allow plenty of time for exploration of ideas, reviewing and planning
- Do not expose them to risk such as by suddenly asking them to engage in an activity
- Are not pressured
- Allow them to stand back from a situation
- Allow them to play a passive role by, for example, observing others take part in a group activity or role-play.

Reflectors may be made to feel uncomfortable if they are encouraged to play a more prominent part in activities or are put under pressure to come up with opinions and ideas. They may feel dissatisfied if a learning situation fails to address things at a deep enough level.

Theorists prefer learning environments which:

- Involve analysis of credible and well-researched theories, models, and systems
- Allow enough time for these to be thoroughly explored and discussed

- Encourage participants to see things from a theoretical standpoint
- Challenge and stimulate intellectually
- Concentrate on objective and logical argument
- Have a clearly defined aim.

Theorists may find learning difficult in situations which appear to lack direction or focus. They may react negatively if asked to analyse things from a subjective or emotional point of view. They will also be uncomfortable if the learning is not based on recognised and accepted thinking, appears contradictory or is not related to theory.

Pragmatists prefer learning environments which:

- Involve new ideas and theories with which the learner is encouraged to experiment
- Have a practical focus and involve learning which can be applied on the job
- Concentrate on subjects, issues or problems they perceive as important or related to an immediate need
- Clearly show the relevance and value of what they are learning
- Include practical guidance and techniques.

Pragmatists may react negatively to activities which appear to lack purpose and, in particular, to situations in which it is unclear that there are practical gains to what they are learning. They may become impatient if placed in a learning activity which involves lengthy debate or analysis, particularly if they feel there is little to be gained.

The above checklist is meant only as a guide to help you to think about what constitutes the most suitable learning environment for you. This should not deter you from seeking out learning situations that involve you in activities which, on the surface, do not immediately suit your preferred learning style.

Knowing what type of learner you are can help you to make the most out of each situation by:

- Encouraging you to find out about the different learning opportunities available in your programme
- Getting you to find out more about what is involved in a learning situation prior to attending
- Helping you to understand why you feel comfortable/uncomfortable in certain situations; this can be very reassuring, particularly if you feel others are responding more or less well than you
- Helping you to make the most of the style of learning you have by being

aware of the strengths and weaknesses that each brings with it
- Enabling you to work constructively on strengthening your weaker areas
- Helping you to make choices as to the type of event you attend
- Helping you to make known your learning preferences to your tutor and other students. This can avoid your being placed in situations which make you feel very uncomfortable or which cause you to have a negative learning experience
- Helping you to seek out extra support when confronted with learning situations which are not compatible with your preferred style of learning.

Endnote

The aim of this chapter has been to give you a deeper understanding of the way in which you learn and the considerations that you will need to take into account during your studies. There is no one right approach to learning; the important thing is to be aware of how you as a learner work best. Your understanding of yourself as a learner is important for you in deciding how to approach your studies and in drawing up learning goals and a study plan. These topics will be explored in the next chapter.

In this chapter we have looked at:

- The personal considerations you need to bear in mind in drawing up your study plan, such as your body rhythms, your need for a healthy diet, sleep and relaxation
- Whether or not you need to make changes in your lifestyle in order to facilitate your learning
- What will keep you going
- Some of your personal learning experiences and what they can tell you about how you prefer to learn
- Some theories about how people learn so that you can make the most of your preferred learning style. You may choose to use other styles when they might be beneficial or in order to develop them.

REFERENCES
1. Entwhistle, N.J., Ramsden, P. *Understanding Student Learning*. London: Croom Helm, 1983; 16–17.
2. Honey, P., Mumford, A. *The Manual of Learning Styles* (3rd edn). Maidenhead, Berkshire: Honey, 1992.

3. Planning and evaluating

Making the most of open learning materials requires planned study and active involvement in all learning decisions. True learning is not just a question of acquiring facts or obtaining knowledge. It must involve an active relationship with what you read and study that leads to some degree of change – in your behaviour, attitudes or skill level, for example.

Setting learning goals and establishing a study plan are essential parts of getting started on your studies. In addition, evaluation of your learning is an important element which will help you to set further learning goals.

Evaluation is discussed later in this chapter. It begins with the process of identifying your personal learning goals.

Setting learning goals

Setting learning goals is an important part of the process of being actively involved in your learning. Learning goals are unique to you and your particular studies. They are independent of any course objectives that have been identified within the learning materials themselves and are for you to decide. Personal learning goals can help you to:

• Motivate yourself by giving you valid reasons for learning
• Establish your learning priorities
• Decide on your study approach
• Take responsibility for your own development
• Integrate your studies with your work
• Become an active learner
• Reflect on your development
• Evaluate the learning experience.

Clearly, learning goals are not just the end result of your studies, such as achieving a degree, but the steps along the way. You need to break down any overall objectives you have into smaller, more manageable chunks.

Some guidelines for you to bear in mind are given in the box below.

Components of learning goals

Learning goals should incorporate:

1. Success criteria – so that you know if and when you have achieved your goals.

2. A time-scale – because open-ended goals have a tendency to drag on or fail to be achieved.

3. Clear and concise language – so that you and others will know exactly what is required.

4. Realistic measures – because you don't want to set yourself up to fail.

5. Relevant content – so that the goals reflect what is most important to you in terms of your learning priorities.

ACTIVITY 1
Write down in two or three sentences what you hope to achieve through your course and how you see it benefiting your professional life.

What, for example, do you want to be able to do, think, feel, understand and know?

How would this learning be recognised by others?

What are the steps you need to take to reach the end result?

Now produce a set of learning goals based on these reflections, using as a guide the criteria given in the box above.

You may have found this Activity difficult to do, particularly if you are unused to taking responsibility for your own learning. However, by formulating goals you have taken the first step towards becoming an independent learner. You will also be in a better position to benefit from the learning experience and to know how to apply your learning personally and professionally.

It is likely that you will want different things from your course at different times. It is important, therefore, that you continually update your learning goals in line with any new priorities as you change and develop.

Establishing a study schedule

Do you find it difficult to get down to studying? Perhaps you find yourself procrastinating – other jobs suddenly take on an urgency or significance they've never had previously and simply have to be tackled before you can start studying. This is a common problem that has been encountered by many students.

Your first learning goal should be to complete a study plan. A suggestion of how this learning goal might look is given in the box below.

Learning goal 1 — Study plan

By the end of the month, I will have produced a realistic study plan for the next year which includes all the relevant study components and time for family, friends, my hobbies and household chores.

My success criteria are that I:

• Keep to the plan
• Feel more organised and less stressed about my studies
• Complete my essays on time
• Continue my swimming, aerobics classes and twice-weekly social events.

A comprehensive study plan should include time for all your activities and help you to focus on your studies at the times allocated to them. Assigning specific times to all the other jobs and distractions that arise will help to ensure that they are tackled only at their allocated times and do not interfere with your study schedule.

A well-thought-out study plan will also take into account *how* you learn, so that you plan to study during the times of the day when you are likely to be at your best.

Your study plan will help you to make long-term decisions about an end-date for completion of your course. Open-ended courses can often lose their sense of urgency so that they drag on indefinitely.

It is important, therefore, that you have an overall plan in mind as to when you want to complete the course and that you use this plan to help you devise a suitable strategy for study.

Fitting studying into an already busy schedule can be difficult and requires careful planning. An important first step is to keep some kind of time-log to help you become aware of what free time you have available and how you spend your time at the moment. This is what you are asked to do for the next Activity. You should carry out this Activity over a two- to three-week period.

ACTIVITY 2
Keep an account, in as much detail as you can, of how you spend your time.

When you have done this, consider whether there are any activities that can be eliminated from your daily or weekly routine to give you more time.

This may involve postponing certain activities, delegating them to others or cutting them out of your life completely.

Analysis of this type can often be revealing because it can illustrate how much time is actually wasted. Conversely, you may find that you simply have too much to do to fit into 24 hours. You can then make decisions as to which particular project or activity to cut out. Remember, however, the story of Peter from Chapter 2, and do not cut out all your leisure, sporting or social activities. They are important in helping you to be at your best when you study.

It is equally important to recognise that you cannot plan every waking minute of your life. As well as planning for free time, you need to allow for contingencies. Giving yourself some 'catch-up' time can be a good idea.

Be honest about the amount of time you need to achieve each activity. This is where the record of how you spent your time will be useful. The more realistic you are, the more chance you have of keeping to your study schedule.

Above all, a good study plan should alleviate your anxieties, not cause them. If you find yourself regularly unable to keep to your plan, this is a sure sign that it is not achievable and needs to be reconsidered. Ultimately, this may mean extending the time in which you complete the course.

The following box lists a number of considerations to bear in mind when planning your schedule. You may be able to identify others for yourself that relate to your particular circumstances.

Revising your schedule

Unless you have experience at planning and sticking to this kind of schedule, it is likely that you won't get it right first time. Do not give up on making a timetable just because the first couple of attempts prove to be unworkable. Analyse what went wrong and revise your schedule accordingly. Finding the right balance of flexibility and control can be difficult, but it is worth persevering. This is an area where you may find it useful to get some support, particularly if you can identify someone who is going through the same process or who has experience of a similar course.

Organising your sequence of study

Many courses that take an open learning approach will include recommended study routes and clear signposting within the core materials. These will normally be broken up into sections and you will usually be given an indication as to whether they need to be studied in a particular order because they relate to each other or whether they are independent and can be studied in any order. If your course is not structured in this way, you may need to spend some time deciding your route through the material you want to cover. You can always seek help with this from your tutor or from other students.

You will also need to take into account any deadline dates for essays, assignments and examinations. How and at what speed you proceed will also depend on your learning goals and priorities as well as on any other requirements the course lays down.

How many study plans?

Bearing all this in mind, you may decide that more than one study plan would be useful. For example, you may want an overall strategy which looks at your studies on an annual basis and includes plans for covering key parts of the course by certain dates. You may then want a more detailed study plan covering a month or a week at a time.

Some examples of different kinds of study plans are given in the Appendix. You may like to photocopy these and use one of them for the next Activity.

ACTIVITY 3
When you feel you are ready and you have completed Activity 2, draw up a study plan. Decide for yourself what period of time you want to cover and bear in mind all the points we have discussed both in this chapter and in Chapter 2.

When you have completed your plan, you might like to get some feedback about it from a tutor, friend or colleague. See how you get on in implementing it – you may want to ask for some support in this – and review it accordingly. Remember that you are in charge of your study plan and not it you, so you can change and adapt it as you discover more about how you learn and the course you are studying. Bear in mind that cultivating a sense of ownership of your own development is an important step towards becoming an independent learner.

It takes time and practice to plan how to study effectively. It will require you to become aware of yourself as a learner and to create study patterns and rituals which work for you. This time is well spent, however, because it will enable you not only to maximise the time you have available, but to enhance greatly your personal effectiveness in the process.

As well as devising learning goals and a study plan, you need to make sure that you regularly evaluate your learning. This will enable you to make the most of your studies and ensure that your learning goals remain relevant, up to date and meaningful. We now look at some of the purposes of evaluation.

The purposes of evaluation

1. Evaluation allows you to learn from past experiences
If a period of study or an assignment goes badly you will want to know why and how this happened so that you can learn from your mistakes. Equally important to your learning, but often forgotten, is the examination of your successes and the factors behind them.

2. Evaluation enables you to prosper from your learning
Study is a quest for growth and increased understanding and unless you

evaluate precisely what and how you have gained from the learning experience, you risk losing much that could have been of value.

A student who had obtained a PhD from Oxford University, for example, decided to draw up a profile because:

'I have been right through the educational system and yet I still have no idea what I have learned from this – what my education means to me'.

3. Evaluation helps keep you on track
Regular checking of your progress against your study plan and learning goals will help to ensure you meet deadlines and achieve your learning outcomes.

4. Evaluation helps you to assess what you have learned and how this can affect your professional and personal life
All learning changes you – your attitudes, skills, knowledge and values. Being able to recognise this is important if you are to benefit in both your personal and professional life.

5. Evaluation helps you make informed choices in line with your development needs
By keeping up to date with your development in terms of what you have learned and how this has changed you, you will be able to update your learning goals and priorities accordingly.

6. Evaluation helps you to remain in control of your own learning
Regular evaluation gives you the opportunity to remind yourself of your learning goals and encourages you to amend these goals in the light of your summative assessments.

Critical reflection

Reflection occurs naturally throughout our lives and we all, to a greater or lesser extent, reflect on things that have happened to us. We tend, however, to focus on events that went badly and to dwell on the incident itself rather than on the learning that occurred.

Analysing or evaluating your learning requires you to draw out the significant learning and consider ways of implementing it in your professional life. This should not be limited to learning related to your study, however. An important feature of open learning is the ability to recognise the potential learning in all situations. This will enable you to benefit from all your experiences and appreciate skills, knowledge and qualities that you may hitherto have undervalued. In addition, by seeing your personal expertise as a resource for professional knowledge, you will be acknowledging the fact that the two are intertwined and inseparable, one informing the other.

How you conduct your professional life, and your values, attitudes and beliefs, are all affected not just by what happens in the workplace, but by your life in general. The reflective process, therefore, needs to take into account all types of experiences.

Critical reflection will help you to:

- Recognise skills, knowledge and qualities hitherto unrecognised but relevant to your course
- Use these skills to inform and enrich your learning
- Change as a result of what you have learned
- Apply these changes in the workplace and life in general.

The reflective process in action

Donald Schön, in *The Reflective Practitioner: How professionals think in action*[1], writes that reflective practice is essential for personal growth:

'... as the professional moves towards new competences, he gives up some familiar sources of satisfaction and opens himself to new ones . . . The new satisfactions open to him are largely about his knowledge in practice, and about himself. When a practitioner becomes a researcher in his own practice, he engages in a continuing process of self-education.'

Reflective practice has, in effect, three parts:

1. Reflecting on an experience
Asking yourself such questions as: What happened? How and why? How did I feel at the time? What about now? What went well/badly?

2. Identifying where significant learning occurred
What could I have done differently? What can I learn from the incident?

3. Giving evidence of that learning
How can I demonstrate my learning? This evidence can be included in your profile and could also give you credit for prior learning.

Keeping a reflective diary

Keeping a reflective diary is a valuable way of encouraging and recording reflective practice. A reflective diary can also assist you in charting your progress and in identifying when learning occurs, both during your studies and beyond.

An example of a reflective diary is given in the box below.

Sample reflective diary

19th June
I am having difficulty producing a study plan which is feasible. There just do not seem to be enough hours in the day and I am not convinced that I can give this course the hours it will require. I'm going to speak to my tutor about this next week, but quite frankly I'm really anxious about the whole thing and feel I may have bitten off more than I can chew.

22nd June
Went out with Sandy last night and discussed the whole course and how I'm feeling. We went over my study plan and he feels I haven't been very scientific in my approach and that I've probably exaggerated the time needed for many things. He recommended that I maintain a time-log for a week to get a better idea of how long I should allocate for each responsibility. I was a bit defensive with him, as I got the distinct impression that he thought I was making excuses and that the real problem is that I just don't want to do the course. This is simply not true – or is it?

23rd July
Well, I've done my time-log and, yes, Sandy was right – I've overestimated quite considerably in a number of areas. The results were quite illuminating, as was the fact that I've not studied at all in the meantime on the pretext that I needed to do my time-log first. I know I've now got to face up to a few difficult decisions. Will I pack the whole thing in or is it time to stop making excuses and get down to some work?

31st July
This is my fourth day of studies and things seem to be working out. And – it's not as bad as I thought it was going to be. Who knows, I might even begin to enjoy it!

ACTIVITY 4
In what ways is this a critical incident for the learner? What learning, if any, can she draw from this experience?

How could this learning be put to good use within her course and her professional and personal life?

The above illustration is an example of a critical incident in that it gives the learner an opportunity to look at herself and the sort of person she is. A critical incident can be:

- An incident in which you were involved directly or one which you observed
- Something that went particularly well
- Something that went badly
- Something that you found particularly challenging
- Something typical or something unusual
- A single event or a series of connected incidents.

Your reflective diary is a useful place to record critical incidents. Some of these you might reflect on immediately, while others may become significant only later. In the latter circumstance it is simply a case of recording the events and your feelings about them as they occur, without attempting to carry out any analysis at this stage.

Critical incident analysis and reflective practice can be particularly useful if tied in with a goal-setting process. This involves making specific goals related to the learning identified by the reflective process and using these to help you put into practice what you have learned.

Reviewing what you have learned

Reviewing your learning at regular and appropriate intervals will enable you to measure your learning as you progress. There are a number of ways you can do this, including the three suggestions given below.

1. *Day-to-day reviews* – by writing in your reflective diary.

2. *Periodic reviews* – to help you chart less dramatic but equally fundamental changes in your knowledge, skills and attitudes. This may also involve reviewing earlier episodes recorded in your diary which have become more meaningful.

3. *A formative review* – at the end of your studies or a major topic. This involves checking that your goals have been met and analysing the impact of the learning on your professional knowledge. You may want to consider your next steps and to start setting further goals. It may also be appropriate to give some feedback about the course to your tutor or the course organisers.

Although there is not the scope in this book to explore reflective practice or develop a portfolio or profile in more depth, there are many excellent publications available, a few of which are listed in the Further Reading section at the end of the book.

Endnote

In this chapter we have looked at a number of activities to help you to make the most of open learning materials:

- Setting personal learning goals – why these are important and what they should contain
- Developing a study schedule – so that you can plan all aspects of your study, including your leisure time
- Evaluating your learning – to enable you to identify your strengths as well as areas for growth
- Using critical reflection and keeping a reflective diary – these will make a significant contribution to your personal and professional development.

REFERENCE

[1] Schön, D. *The Reflective Practitioner: How professionals think in action.* Aldershot: Avebury Press, 1991.

4. Making the most of the resources available

This chapter looks first at the range of resources, including people, that are available to you and how you can make the most of them. It then explores the learning resources available in open learning courses and how these affect the way you learn. Even if you are not studying by open learning, you will still find this discussion relevant.

Creating the right environment

As an adult learner, it is likely that most of your studying is done at home where the environment may be less than ideal. Conditions will vary enormously, from having a dedicated study room to a dedicated armchair! If you are in the latter situation and have to put all your books and materials away after each study period, you will know how time-consuming and offputting this can be. However, there is no such thing as an ideal learning environment. As with learning methods, whatever works for you is the best way to learn.

Susan's preferred learning environment

Susan is an ex-student who has been right through the educational and professional qualifications system. She carried out nearly all of her studying, including reading, writing notes, revising and writing essays, sitting in front of the television with her family all around her.

On pressure from her family, who felt sure she couldn't possibly concentrate with all the noise, she tried to work in her bedroom and hated it! She simply wasn't able to sit in silence or in isolation from everyone else as this made her feel cut off. Having noise and people around her were positive aids to her concentration.

She still works best this way and much prefers an open-plan environment to that of a separate office, so much so that her colleagues sitting near her no longer book a meeting room when they need to get together. They know that she won't be distracted by their conversation and actually prefers to have people around her.

Susan may be unusual, but her experience illustrates the point that different environments help or hinder concentration levels and that you need to be sure that you have the right setting for yourself.

ACTIVITY 1
Picture your ideal learning environment in as much detail as you can, then ask yourself the following questions:

- **Does it have any background noise such as music playing?**
- **Are there other people around? If so, where are they and what are they doing?**
- **How have you organised your study materials? Where are all your materials and how tidy is the room?**
- **What other equipment do you have?**
- **What type of chair is there?**
- **How warm or cold is it ?**
- **Whereabouts are you in relation to the door and window?**

Now consider where you are studying at the moment. Is there anything you can do to make it closer to your ideal learning environment?

It may be that you use different environments for different activities. You might, for example, use a library when you are writing an essay so that you have a quiet environment and access to materials as you work. If circumstances restrict your choice of where to study, it is important to plan how you will use your study time in order to maximise its effectiveness. You may need to make compromises between what is possible and what is ideal, but by planning at an early stage you will be able to ensure you have considered all available options and are making the best use of time and resources.

Making the most of tutor support

Most courses include some form of tutor support. You may be asked to attend face-to-face tutorials, either on a one-to-one basis or as part of a group. Your tutor may also provide you with written feedback on each piece of work submitted and may be available (often at set times of the day or week) for you to contact for additional advice and support.

On an open learning course, how and to what extent you use your tutor will usually be largely left up to you to decide. This may be very different from what you have been used to in the past. Your relationship with your tutor is a partnership of equals and it is his/her job to provide you with the kind of support and guidance that is appropriate for your individual needs. It is your responsibility as an independent learner, however, to ensure that this happens. Your tutor will naturally presume, for example, that you are happy with the amount of written feedback given on your assignments unless you indicate otherwise. On the other hand, your tutor will be happy to expand on this and give you additional advice if you request it.

Being well prepared in terms of knowing what you want from your tutor – including having prepared a set of questions to ask and having the relevant material, page numbers and so on to hand – will help you achieve the most from any contact, be it face-to-face or over the telephone.

Learning from other people

Learning from other people is just as important in your studies as it is in your work and life in general. You may not be aware of it, but all of us have an immense pool of untapped resources in terms of the people around us. These are not just your tutors or the subject matter experts that you know; they include people who may be younger or less experienced than yourself, but who can, in one way or another, give you different kinds of support.

ACTIVITY 2
Make a list of the people who might be helpful to you in your learning.

Think about the ways in which you would like these people to support you. For example, you may want your manager to help negotiate access to other work areas. Make a note of when and in what way you will approach them.

Your list probably includes people who can help in both academic and non-academic ways. For example, you may want your family's support in terms of practical help and giving you time and space to study without being interrupted. In these circumstances you will be asking for their understanding and tolerance more than anything else. The same may also be required of your colleagues, some of whom will be more supportive than others. They may feel threatened – aware that they are not keeping up with new developments professionally and anxious that your new knowledge and skills will overshadow theirs or expose their inadequacies. You could allay their anxieties by discussing your course with them and sharing what you are doing in order to help them overcome their fears. In return, you stand to benefit from their experience and help in relating what you are learning to your practice.

We mentioned briefly the importance of student networking. Even if it is not possible to set up support groups which meet on a face-to-face basis, regular telephone contact can be of enormous benefit in providing mutual support and the opportunity to exchange ideas. Some open learning courses include the facility to network via computer conferencing.

Support groups can be used to:

• Debate issues and topics
• Give mutual support
• Share revision notes/reading/general note-taking/book reviews
• Pass on new information/research/developments.

Did you put librarians on the list of people who could help you in Activity 2? We now discuss how to make the most of the services offered by libraries.

Using libraries effectively

Even if you are on an open learning course that provides the core materials, you will need to supplement these with additional reading. Most of this material will probably be sourced through the library network.

The following types of libraries are available:

• Large town/city libraries usually contain comprehensive collections, including archives, with a good selection of materials in certain areas such as the humanities, business, education and the social sciences

• Local public libraries vary enormously in size and may be of limited use to you in your studies. However, the inter-library loan service makes it possible for you to borrow books which are not in the local library

- University/college libraries are geared to academic study and carry a large selection of materials, including multiple copies of key books relating to individual subject areas. Even if you are not attached to the academic institution served by the library, it is often possible to visit it and borrow books as a visiting student. Where there are specialised sections relating to your subject area, you are likely to find that the staff are able to provide you with guidance and help about the materials you require

- There may be other specialist libraries in your field. In health care there are nursing and medical libraries, or, increasingly, a combination of the two, which cater for the medical, nursing and allied health professions. Membership may be limited to particular hospital or community trust employees, but if you ask you will almost certainly be allowed to use these libraries for reference purposes. You may also be able to join as an external member and pay a fee which allows you to use all the library facilities

- Government departmental libraries and specialist collections (such as a history society library) are usually accessible only by special request.

As you can see from the above list, you will normally have access to more than one library, and which you use most often will probably depend on practical constraints as well as what your primary needs are. It may be, for example, that you decide to use the larger libraries for research or to borrow particular texts, but that you still prefer to work in the smaller local library, not just because of its location but because you feel more at ease there.

There are three main steps to using libraries effectively:

- Knowing what materials the library contains
- Knowing how to access relevant materials
- Choosing relevant sources.

Selecting and sourcing your reading material is covered in Chapter 5.

Knowing what materials libraries contain and how to access them

Libraries contain a mass of useful information, equipment and materials, but it may not be readily apparent what is available that is appropriate for you. Few of us can easily access the full range of resources without some degree of assistance with the specific systems, procedures and layout used by that particular library. Some libraries, especially those linked to academic institutions, provide students with a guided tour, and it is a good idea to take this opportunity if at all possible. However, every library is likely to have a leaflet which includes, for instance, a breakdown of the services available, times of opening and a layout map. Reading this through carefully and spending some time just walking round and familiarising yourself with where things are located and what is available can save you time and trouble later.

Librarians are usually extremely helpful and willing to assist you. They have extensive knowledge of their library's holdings and know how to obtain information their library does not have. They are an invaluable resource that you should not overlook.

Much of the vast wealth of information available is in the form of textbooks, but other sources are also useful and are often under-utilised by students. Your library may have pamphlets, copies of government publications, periodicals, encyclopaedias, research papers, dissertations, almanacs, abstracts, microfilm of old newspapers, audio-cassettes, photographs, drawings and paintings, some of which may be very valuable sources of learning to you. Magazines and journals, in particular, provide up-to-date information, sources, ideas and research findings.

Finding your way around

Accessing the information you need will require you to familiarise yourself with the systems used by your particular library for cataloguing, classifying, indexing and shelving. The method of shelving materials such as pamphlets and large and valuable books, for example, may differ between libraries, as will the allocation of items to subject classifications in catalogues and indexes. Again, the librarians will be able to help you become familiar with these.

Libraries usually list the books on their shelves in catalogues or indexes under the headings of subject, author and title. These indexes used to be on cards, filed alphabetically, but these days microfiche or computer are used virtually everywhere. Computerised catalogues are by far the quickest way to locate the materials you require.

Whatever the system in operation, it will provide you with further information on the item, including its location in the library and shelf number. You need to make sure you fully understand the system operating in all the libraries you use.

The journals that your library takes will generally be listed separately. Usually the most recent issues are prominently displayed, with back issues filed under the journal title in the relevant section of the library.

Specialist databases on CD-ROM are an ever-increasing feature of all types of library and an invaluable source of current information. They provide facilities which enable you to search for relevant journal articles by author, publication year, country of publication, title, key words or subject area. These features can be combined to enable you to search very specifically or they can be used individually to give an overview of what has been published recently in your field.

The databases held in your library may be kept on open access or you may be able to book a session on the CD-ROM. Your librarian will be happy to teach you how to gain the most from this search tool.

How confident are you that you are utilising your library to the full and that you know your way around it? If you are in any doubt, then tackle the next Activity.

ACTIVITY 3
Do you know how to find out if your library holds the book that you want, even if you have only part of the information about it, such as the author but not the title?

Are you sure you know what resources (not just books) your library contains that could be of use to you?

What CD-ROM databases relevant to your field does your library hold and what subjects to they cover?

If you are working on a particular subject, perhaps for an essay, do you know how to access all the material available, not only that which is held in the library itself?

If you are not clear about any of the points raised in this Activity, talk to one of the librarians so that you do not waste a valuable resource.

What learning media are available?

The written word is not the only means of learning, particularly on an open learning course. There may be local or national events such as talks, conferences or exhibitions which cover a topic that is relevant to your studies. These can be very useful in bringing your subject to life, particularly if they give you the opportunity to meet subject matter experts.

Other learning methods include:

- Lectures
- Tutorials/seminars/workshops
- Audio-tapes/radio/television
- Slides
- Video
- Computer conferencing facilities/computer-based training (CBT) packages.

Such a variety of learning media means that you need to be flexible and adapt your approach accordingly. Some of the learning media that may be available to you are discussed below.

Open learning materials

The learning medium used in most open/distance learning courses is text. Open learning texts will include exercises or Activities which serve to replace face-to-face classroom discussions. These Activities are usually followed by a commentary or guidance as to the main learning points of the Activity and/or how the work you have done can be applied to the topic under review. The Activities offer a wide range of learning opportunities and you may be asked to read, reflect, inquire, write, discuss with colleagues or carry out tasks.

Such Activities will help you in:

1. *Building a knowledge base*
   You may be asked to read some factual information and then to extract important points. Subsequent feedback may then list the salient points that you could have identified.

2. *Undertaking critical analysis*
   You may be presented with a series of contrasting theories and arguments to stimulate a debate in your mind. An Activity might then ask you to analyse these and the commentary will provide feedback on the main points that you could have made.

3. *Applying theory to practice*
   You may be asked to reflect on a range of ideas, opinions or research

findings and then relate them to your personal experience. You may be encouraged to carry out follow-up action which is designed to show you alternative approaches.

4. *Examining attitudes and emotions*

You may be asked to identify your own feelings, for example, where you stand in relation to opposing attitudes. Acknowledging your attitudes is an important step in the learning process, and is often easier to achieve in an open learning environment. Once you have identified and acknowledged your attitudes and feelings, you will be able to assess and possibly change them.

Lectures

The value of lectures is fiercely debated in the academic world and, as with most things, there are both pros and cons. A good lecturer can bring a subject alive for the learner. When the main medium is the written word it can be very refreshing to hear your subject being talked about, particularly by an expert in the field.

By following the lecturer's train of thought, you can also see how to develop an argument. In addition, you will benefit from up-to-date information and an analysis of new developments, research or thinking.

Although not a primary learning method for open learners, many open courses do include the provision for students to attend lectures. These can have a variety of different functions, but are often developed to provide subject-specific guidance, particularly in areas that have traditionally caused students problems.

Other lectures may give an overview of a particular subject or provide guidance on study skills such as writing essays. Attendance at a lecture will also provide you with an ideal opportunity to make contact with other learners.

There are, however, certain difficulties that can be experienced by learners with this medium. As you are normally afforded only one chance to hear a lecture, it can be difficult to strike a balance between wanting to take as many notes as possible and concentrating fully on following the lecturer's argument. It is all too easy to miss the main points or gist of what is being said, or to lose track of the overall flow of the argument in an attempt to record everything. This is also true if you lose your concentration for a while, when it may be difficult for you to catch up, particularly where understanding of later sections relies on having assimilated what has gone before. Some techniques for getting the most out of a lecture include:

1. Take a tape-recorder and record the lecture (ask the lecturer's permission beforehand).

2. Pair up with another student and exchange notes.

3. Establish what you want from the lecture before you attend it and concentrate on those parts which are relevant to your specific interests. It can be helpful to rephrase your objectives into a series of questions.

4. Focus on distinguishing between major and minor points.

5. Review what you already know and where this lecture fits into the overall subject area. (This will help you to avoid taking unnecessary notes.)

6. Reflect on the lecture and re-read your notes before the end of the day; this will help you retain more of the learning content. Make links between these notes and others, annotating where relevant, and file them in the appropriate place.

7. Don't take what the lecturer says at face value. Actively listen and question what you are hearing. In particular, try to consider:

- What are the main ideas being put forward?
- What, if any, is the lecturer's bias?
- How does what is being said compare with what you already know, think and feel about the subject?
- Are the arguments being put forward sound? Are they based on any evidence?
- Does the argument flow logically?
- Are there alternative conclusions or viewpoints that could be put forward?
- Are there any gaps or flaws in what is being put forward?
- How does the content apply to your course or professional life?

These are the sorts of questions that you need to consider when using any of the learning media accessed during your course.

Adopting a questioning stance helps you to develop your skills as an independent learner and to reflect critically on the value of what you are studying. This is an essential technique for studying at a higher level as well as for ensuring that you are able to derive full benefit from what you have learned.

Working in small groups

You may have a number of opportunities for working in small groups during tutorials, seminars or workshops that are held as part of your course. These can vary widely in structure and content.

Group work may take any of the following forms:
- Individual discussions with your personal tutor on your progress, including feedback on any written assignments that you have submitted for assessment
- Group discussions or debate on particular aspects of the course or on new developments/research
- Group-led sessions where the tutor remains relatively unobtrusive and the learners themselves set the agenda
- Role-playing or group activities to practise certain skills or to apply some of the learning content from the course
- Mini-lectures by the tutor or other members of the group.

The benefits of attending group sessions are numerous. They can help to clarify your ideas and feelings on a subject or clear up any confusion that you are experiencing with certain areas of the learning material.

Group sessions can also help to develop your communication skills and analytical abilities by providing opportunities for debate and the exchange of ideas with fellow learners and tutors. For many learners, tutorials and group work are a welcome break from solitary study. In addition, being in a group can help to alleviate any feelings of self-doubt. It is reassuring to meet other students and to find that they have the same doubts and worries as yourself.

The principles and techniques relating to group sessions are, in essence, those which apply to every learning situation. If you are to enjoy and learn from group sessions, you need to prepare for them beforehand, participate actively during them and carry out a review of the learning gained, preferably later the same day.

Preparing for group sessions

If you prepare well for a group session you will stand a much better chance of being able to participate fully and having your learning needs met.

Before attending the tutorial or seminar you need to have as clear a picture as possible of what the overall aims and proposed content of the day are. This will give you the opportunity to read up on the subject under review and highlight any particular areas that you do not understand or about which you require further clarification.

Your preparatory reading will normally involve you in reviewing your notes, the course materials, perhaps some background reading or a previous essay on the subject. You may have been given some exercises to do by your tutor, who might also have given you specific reading material or general guidance as to how you can best prepare.

This type of preparation will help you to develop your own views and ideas about the subject area. Where the content of the day is open and left to the group members to decide, this sort of preparation is vital.

As with reading or attending lectures, having a set of questions which you would like answered during the seminar or tutorial will also help you to formulate your desired learning outcomes for the day and ensure that your particular needs are met.

When no preparatory work is specified, you may be tempted not to bother. Even then, however, it is worthwhile preparing so that you are not spending most of the time trying to absorb material which you have forgotten or which is readily available at home. Instead, endeavour to see group events as invaluable opportunities to:

- Develop your evaluative and critical analysis skills
- Gain a deeper understanding of your subject area, including the different ways it can be approached
- Formulate your own views
- Get to grips with any aspects of the subject that have been causing you particular problems
- Improve your communication skills
- Find out about new developments in your subject area, such as current research, legislation
- Gain feedback on your performance/progress
- Enjoy a collective educational experience
- Form links with other learners.

Taking an active part in group work

Sunita's experience

Sunita, a very bright and enthusiastic degree student, was delighted when the rest of her group asked her to be team leader for one of the exercises at a workshop she was attending. The exercise went very well and she was pleased with her performance.

She knew that she had a tendency to dominate things, however, and so, after chatting to her tutor during the break, agreed that she would take a bit more of a back seat during questions and the next exercise.

To her surprise (and secret delight!) the group volunteered her again as leader for the next exercise. However, she suggested that this wouldn't be fair and insisted that someone else should have the chance to be group leader. This was reluctantly accepted by the group and after some discussion another group member was chosen.

This time the exercise didn't go as well and Sunita found herself having to step in more and more in order to get the group better organised. Everything got very chaotic towards the end, with several people being asked to do the same thing and others doing nothing and, in Sunita's eyes, simply giving up.

The debriefing following the exercise was very difficult for Sunita as she found herself, to her amazement, under attack by the rest of the group who seemed to be blaming her for what had gone wrong.

ACTIVITY 4

Get together with a group of colleagues or fellow students to do this Activity.

Using the following questions as a springboard, discuss what happened to Sunita and compare it with your experience of working in groups:

- **What might be some of the criticisms levelled at Sunita?**
- **Why did the group blame her for what went wrong?**
- **Why did the group ask her to be team leader again?**
- **How does your knowledge of learning styles (from Chapter 2) explain Sunita's behaviour?**
- **If you were in Sunita's position, how might you have responded at each stage and what might have been the outcome for the group?**
- **What could Sunita have learnt from the exercise?**
- **What have you discovered from this Activity about yourself as a group member?**

Recollect the last three team events you attended – perhaps a staff meeting, a team effort at work, a case study, seminar or tutorial. How do these recollections compare with your thoughts about yourself as a group member?

The example of Sunita is designed to show the difficulties which can occur when someone tries to adopt a group role which is out of character.

Sunita, for the best of reasons, tried to take more of a back seat for the second exercise and, had everything gone well, she may have succeeded and managed to curb her natural Activist inclination to take charge. However, as the exercise was not fitting in with her picture of how it should be, she was unable to stop herself from continually interfering and trying to impose herself and her own ideas onto the group. She effectively undermined the new leader's authority and, with two people issuing separate instructions, things just went from bad to worse. So what were the choices available to Sunita?

She could have accepted the initial group pressure to continue as group leader and she may have led them to success the second time round. However, this would have denied the others the opportunity to try a new role or to experience the impact that a change in group dynamics can have on the way a team works together. Also, it would not have allowed Sunita the opportunity to practise being a team member, which, judging from how things turned out, is something she finds difficult to do.

As this was a learning situation, it was important that the group members were encouraged not to rely on one person. The exercise was more concerned with exploring the issues surrounding teamwork than with completing the actual task set. Even though, or perhaps because of, the fact that the group failed to achieve the task set, this was a very valuable, albeit probably painful, learning experience for all, particularly Sunita.

Having chosen to relinquish the leadership, Sunita should have accepted the fact that things would not be run as she might wish and that her role was to support the new leader. This is not to say she couldn't have contributed her ideas and suggestions; however, she had to be particularly careful about the way she did so, knowing her tendency to dominate things.

As you can see from this example, it is important that we are aware of how we tend to behave in group situations and, in particular, of the positive and negative aspects of our behaviour.

How you respond in a group situation will depend on many factors, including whether you know the group already and feel comfortable with its members, the number of people present, your reactions to the tutor, and how confident you feel about the approach to be taken and the subject in question (which is why being fully prepared is so important). Where there are likely to be role-playing exercises, you may feel more anxious and less willing to participate than if asked to join a group debate on a subject you know well. Other factors, such as how you are feeling on the day and whether you have any other worries or problems, are also likely to influence how you respond to a group situation.

You will remember from the discussion of learning styles in Chapter 2 that knowing the type of learner you are will help you to be aware of how you learn best and in what areas you need to stretch yourself in order to get the most out of a learning situation. It is often difficult to change your learning style, as Sunita discovered, but it can widen the range of what you learn. This may involve you in one of the following:

• Learning to take a back seat at times
• Ensuring you do contribute your ideas and opinions
• Listening to others even when you don't agree with what is being said
• Understanding that it is natural to feel uncertain at times and that we can all help one another in these situations by showing mutual respect and understanding.

Listening skills will be looked at in the next chapter.

Endnote

In this chapter we have seen that there are a multitude of resources available to the open as well as the traditional learner. Some are more readily available than others but each requires you, the learner, to take responsibility for making the best of what is on offer.

It may be possible for you to achieve success by limiting yourself to working through the course material. If you are to benefit fully from the learning experience, however, you should seek to enrich and supplement your learning in as many ways as possible. Attending exhibitions, talks, self-help groups, tutorials and seminars, as well as discussing your work with colleagues, your family and friends will all help to bring your subject alive and to give it meaning for you in your personal and professional life.

In this chapter we have explored:

• How to create an appropriate environment for study
• How to make the most of your tutor
• The value of learning from other people
• How to use libraries effectively
• Making the most of the learning resources available, including lectures and group work.

5. Reading and listening skills

Approaching reading

Starting at the beginning is often the most logical approach when faced with something new. When you read a novel, for example, you start at page one and carry on until you reach the end. However, this is generally not the best way to approach academic study, where a different style of reading is required.

You are likely, for instance, to have at least some degree of knowledge already, so you could be wasting time or undervaluing your previous experience by reading material from beginning to end. You may also find that you get bogged down in material that is not directly relevant.

This is not to say that you can never read academic material for pure enjoyment; when you find something of particular interest, you may want to read it straight through. It will more often be the case, however, that your time is limited, that you need to focus on a particular line of enquiry – perhaps you are working towards a deadline date for an assignment – and that you need to keep purpose and direction in your reading.

Many students find the sheer volume of their course reading matter overwhelming and this is one of the main reasons why so many fail to enrich their learning through additional reading. Yet degree-level study is known as 'reading' for a degree. Perhaps you believe that you do not need to be selective in what you read or to make use of additional materials because your core materials include everything you need to know; but no course of study is ever designed to give you all the answers or to tell you how you should think, however comprehensive the materials might seem to be. Rather, your study materials are designed to present a range of ideas and theories for you to consider, compare and evaluate, and to stimulate you to explore further.

The ability to reflect critically on all you read is therefore instrumental to the learning process and is a requirement of all degree-level students.

Supplementary and background reading is, therefore, an essential aspect of any study course, and the ability to evaluate different texts and authors is important in order to maximise the benefit that such reading can bring. Many authors are, in effect, expressing the same ideas and differ only superficially in the points that they are making or in how these are expressed.

Your reading materials

The first step in approaching reading is to become aware of what reading materials are available to you. These include:

1. The open learning course materials
These should be written and presented in a clear and accessible way so that they are easy for you to follow and learn from.

2. Textbooks
As these also have been written for students, they will take into account the fact that the reader is learning. They often contain a diversity of opinion rather than just one writer's opinion or work.

3. Research reports
These are aimed at interested professionals and give very detailed information on the specific topic area. They tend to go into much greater detail than is required by most students.

4. Professional/trade journals
These are very useful for obtaining up-to-date information on new developments and thinking. They will often include a specific section for students and cover highly topical issues.

5. Newspapers and magazines
These will provide up-to-date information but usually with less detail, and with less regularity, than is found in professional journals.

ACTIVITY 1
Do you use all of these sources as fully as you could? Make a note of what your main reading materials are and in what way you might be able to widen your selection.

Once you have established what the available materials are, in order to gain the most from your reading you need to:

- Establish your purpose for reading
- Select which material to use
- Decide on the best approach.

Establishing your purpose

As you work through your course you will need to read for a number of different purposes. Let us look now at what some of these might be.

1. As part of the course requirements
Clearly, any reading set as part of the course should have a high priority and your purpose will be to fulfil the course requirements.

2. To gain an overview of your subject
This enables you to place your subject in context or see your subject in a wider framework before you begin to focus on specific areas. If you are a serialist learner (see Chapter 2), this is particularly important. Such reading may include a potted history of your subject, including the major developments that have occurred since its evolution. You may also find it useful to read up on any controversies surrounding it, including contrasting theories and opinions.

3. General or background reading
You will need to supplement your core materials by carrying out some additional reading. When you are not working towards a particular assignment, however, there is a danger that this reading will not be focused. One way of avoiding this it to use your background reading for very specific purposes, such as:

- To reinforce study already carried out
- To prepare for work in a new area or subject
- To gain a deeper understanding or a new perspective on areas of your study that are causing you problems.

Planning your background reading will make it even more valuable to you.

4. To prepare for an assignment
In this case you will have a very clear idea of what you want to read, and why. You may, for example, be reading to find a specific piece of information or to follow a particular argument. Alternatively, you may want to gain up-to-date information on something or compare one viewpoint with another.

5. For enjoyment

You may, of course, find one area of your subject particularly interesting or illuminating and want to follow it up without a specific aim in mind. Be careful, however, that you do not use it to avoid tackling an assignment or your course work.

ACTIVITY 2
Think about your recent and current reading.

What are the purposes of the reading?

Do you feel you do the right amount of background or overview reading, and is it sufficiently focused?

If not, make some notes on how you might redress this. You might allow more time for background reading or ensure that you list the specific purpose of each piece of reading you undertake.

Selecting your material

As it is not practical to attempt to work through each piece of reading material as thoroughly as you would the core text, you will need to make your reading as efficient and effective as possible.

The first step is to be selective about what you read. The following list suggests ways in which you might tackle this.

1. Ask your tutor to recommend specific texts
There may be a reading list supplied as part of the course or one that your tutor can let you have. As these tend to be wide-ranging, you might like to ask your tutor to recommend specific texts for specific purposes.

Do not feel, however, that you have to read recommended texts if you don't get on with them. Not all books that contain good ideas are written in inaccessible language and you do not need to give yourself the hard time of trudging through incomprehensible prose. Choose texts that you find easy to read.

2. Ask fellow students, past and present
Other students may be your most valuable resource as they will have direct experience of how useful, up to date and relevant the material is.

3. Share the reading with other students
Setting up self-help groups is a recognised aid to learning. By sharing the reading you will be able to derive benefit from a far wider range of material than would otherwise be possible.

You may decide to nominate individual members of the group to read certain materials and then to report back to the rest of the group on the usefulness of the material and the main points covered within it.

4. Note down recommendations or references to other sources in your current reading
Not all references will be useful, but where you have found the book itself illuminating it is likely that any recommendation by the author will be of equal quality.

5. Ask your colleagues or managers
They may be aware of new developments and research papers or have a selection of reading matter and journals which might be of value.

6. Ask librarians
Librarians are extremely useful in locating material not immediately available or apparent and in giving advice regarding new publications.

7. Survey textbooks before reading them
Previewing potential reading material is a very useful way of assessing whether and to what degree a particular text is worth reading. This method is also invaluable when you are making a choice between a number of different books covering the same subject. You can also look to see how a topic you know about is covered in a book in order to give you an idea of how well other topics might be handled.

An old saying advises us not to judge a book by its cover, but you don't want to waste time ploughing through material which is badly written, out of date or irrelevant to your overall purpose.

One way of making your reading more effective is to preview potential reading material against a set of pre-determined criteria. In other words, if you know what you want from a book beforehand, then you will be able to assess more easily whether or not it will be of use to you.

The book preview checklist in the following box lists the sorts of questions and criteria that you may want to take into account when you are previewing potential reading material.

Book preview checklist

The author
- Who is the author and is she/he a recognised authority in this field?
- What nationality is the author and does this matter?
- What qualifications/experience does the author have in this area?
- Have you read anything else by the author and what did you think of it?
- Is the book or author on your recommended reading list or on further reading/reference lists of other textbooks?

Publishers
- Who are the publishers?
- When was the book first published?
- How many times has it been reprinted?
- What edition is the book?
- Is it sufficiently up to date?

Contents page
- How much of the book will be of value to you?
- How do the contents relate to your purpose and the other materials you are reading in relation to this subject?

Glossary
- Does the glossary, if there is one, indicate a level which is appropriate for your purposes?

Index
- Does the book appear to cover the appropriate areas and in sufficient depth?

Body of text
- How clear does the language appear to be?
- Is the book well signposted in terms of headings, subheadings, and so on?
- How well structured does it appear to be?
- Will it be easy for you to read?
- Do the chapter introductions and conclusions suggest relevant content?
- Does the level seem appropriate?
- Are there charts/diagrams and how helpful do they seem?

Bibliography/references
- Do they suggest that this book will be suitable for your purposes?
- Are you familiar with any of them?

This type of preview should help you to get a feel for a book – its style, structure and content.

You may now be thinking that there is so much to look at in order to assess a book that you might as well read the whole thing! However, it should not, in reality, take more than a few minutes and you will find yourself doing much of this automatically anyway, each time you pick up a book for the first time.

Deciding on your approach

Your purpose in reading will vary as you progress through your course and this needs to be reflected in the approach that you take. You may, for example, start your study of a particular subject by reading to gain a basic understanding and then go into certain aspects in more detail or from a particular angle. You therefore need to be constantly reminding yourself of your aims so that you will recognise potentially relevant material and adapt what you are reading to serve your purpose. Your approach needs to be appropriate to your purpose in undertaking the reading.

Developing a multi-stage approach to reading

Except in the few circumstances where you want to read straight through a text once only, the most effective and efficient method is to take a multi-stage approach. This involves:

- Conducting an overview of the material
- Framing a set of questions in line with your reading goals
- Reading selected parts of the text
- Taking notes
- Reviewing your reading.

A multi-stage approach offers a number of benefits, as follows:

- It enables you to plan your reading and note-taking in line with your overall goals
- It can save you time by enabling you to concentrate on particular areas of relevance
- It helps you gain an overall understanding of a subject prior to more detailed inspection of particular aspects. This can be particularly helpful if you have a serialist approach to your studies (see Chapter 2)
- It requires you to participate actively during your reading which will help you to remain interested and to evaluate critically what you are studying.

Let us look at each of the stages in turn.

1. Conducting an overview of the material

This is the same technique as the one we have just discussed for previewing a book, and it enables you to gain a broad overview of the materials prior to more systematic study. It involves glancing through the main features of the book or article – for example, the introduction, conclusion, contents page, main headings, diagrams and illustrations – in order to get a feel for what it is about, the main topics covered and the areas on which you want to concentrate your efforts.

2. Framing a set of questions in line with your reading goals
This stage involves formulating some questions about the reading material – perhaps regarding the main arguments put forward, for example, or to gain an understanding of a particular process or philosophy. Clearly, these questions will depend on your reading goals and the particular material you are reading, but a general example might be: 'How does this author's opinion about X (a specific topic) differ from Y's (another author's)?'

When you are studying the core open/distance learning materials, the Activities and questions within the materials themselves will, to a large extent, do this process for you. These Activities and questions will help you check your understanding and apply your learning in the workplace. When you are studying other texts, the questions you devise are a good stimulus to learning and can help to ensure that you are actively participating in the process. They give a purpose to your study and help you look for the meaning behind what you are reading.

3. Reading selected parts of the text
This stage is a more systematic study of those parts of the material that you have identified as being relevant to your reading goals. It involves searching for the answers to your questions and critically evaluating what the writer is saying. It is a good idea not to take notes at this stage so that you can concentrate your efforts on gaining a thorough understanding of the material.

As you tackle this process, you need to keep your mind open to what you are reading and actively look for what is being expressed in the text rather than just reading the words themselves. It is very easy when reading material to focus on surface details or the memorisation of facts. However, there are many clues available within the text itself which point to the real meaning and significance of what is being said. You should aim to distinguish between opinion or prejudice and fact, and be conscious of what your own prejudices are. This 'active reading' will encourage you to look for the main ideas or details being covered (that is, the hierarchy of ideas) and help you to distinguish between facts and the writer's bias or opinion.

Even in texts that seem the most haphazard, however, the writer will often leave a number of different signposts to indicate the main points or themes in the text, or there may be a particular pattern to the way the ideas are organised. Perhaps each chapter begins with the main idea, or one main point may be included within each paragraph. Look out for emphasis – italics, capitals or underlining. The heading titles may also be very useful in identifying the main focus of a particular section.

Where diagrams or charts are used, it can be easy to ignore them. You may, for example, view them as an unwelcome interruption or find them more difficult to read than the text itself. They are there for a purpose, however, and ignoring them or assuming the same information is covered within the core text may result in your losing important details. In addition, they could help you to understand concepts which are difficult to express in words and to appreciate the overall context of what is being covered. As with the main body of text, therefore, they need to be studied carefully.

4. Taking notes
In this stage you make notes on what you have remembered that is relevant to you, preferably without looking at the text itself. This process helps you to focus specifically on what is important to you, enabling you to make notes in your own words rather than being tempted to copy the text, and it is a valuable check that you have understood the material. It may not always be possible to do this, for example where the material contains a lot of factual or detailed information, but if you are able to, it will help you to assess how much information you have taken in and the level of understanding you have achieved. Note-taking is discussed in depth in the next chapter.

5. Reviewing your reading
This stage involves comparing what you have recalled with the text itself and then following up any areas or points that you have missed. You will also want to check that your reading goals and questions have been answered and again carry out any follow-up action required.

Adapting your approach
The actual extent to which you carry out each stage will ultimately depend on your overall purpose. For example, you can aim to extract specific information from the text and focus on this in the reading stage. In these circumstances, however, you need to be careful that you don't misinterpret the information through failure to read enough of the text; the survey stage should help to avoid this. You can also adapt the technique if you need to – for instance when you are reading to help you prepare for an essay – by reducing the time spent on the recall and review stages, and writing notes as you work through the reading stage. But, if you do this, beware of copying down unnecessary material.

There are, however, certain situations where it is important to get a feel for a whole piece of writing in order to capture initial reactions and feelings – perhaps when reading a case study or a narrated event in an article – and in these cases a one-stage approach is more appropriate.

ACTIVITY 3
Select a piece of reading and try out the multi-stage approach. How did this compare with your normal approach? Did you feel you were able to recall more of the relevant content than usual?

Speed reading

The best way to reduce the time taken up by reading is to be more selective about the material you study and then to vary your reading rate in line with your reading goals. This may mean skimming quickly to search for relevant information for an essay, or, conversely, carefully and slowly reading materials which are core or central to your course. Your main preoccupation should be that of comprehension. Speed reading can only be advantageous to you if it doesn't result in your compromising your ability to understand and recall as fully as you need to.

Active listening

We end this chapter by looking at listening skills and the dangers of making assumptions.

Listening and reading skills are related because learning by listening can be just as important in a course of study as learning by reading. In the course of your learning you may listen to lectures, audio-tapes, fellow students, clients, tutors or other people. We saw earlier how significant learning from others in groups can be when we considered the experience of Sunita (Chapter 4), and there have been several Activities that have asked you to share experiences with others as part of your learning.

Just as it is important to keep an open mind in your reading, so, too, is keeping an open mind in your listening important so that you don't jump to the wrong conclusion or miss valuable learning.

Listening to others

This may seem rather obvious, but in reality few of us listen well all of the time and most of us can improve our techniques in this area. Listening is always important, but especially when:

- You are forming a view about something
- You are about to disagree with another person's viewpoint
- Another person wishes to discuss something of a sensitive or personal nature
- Another person is trying to formulate his/her own ideas and feelings
- A new concept or idea is raised.

As with reading, listening should not be a passive activity. Active listening is an important skill to develop if we are to have our own assumptions and views challenged in order that we can grow.

Some of the things involved in active listening are:

- Showing the speaker that you are interested and attentive
- Listening to the ideas being expressed through the words, rather than just the words themselves
- Trying to distinguish between opinion/prejudice and fact
- Refusing to respond to distractions
- Being conscious of your prejudices – keeping an open mind might not be easy if you really disagree, but is vital if you are to evaluate what is being said
- Letting the speaker finish what he or she is saying – if you make assumptions as to what is coming next you may not be right and you could lose some valuable information or insights
- Occasionally contributing a well-thought-out remark or question as appropriate (but not simply waiting for the chance to cut in)
- Expressing support and agreement for an idea that someone else has put forward
- Asking open, rather than closed questions (these are questions which begin with 'what', 'where', 'why', 'how', 'who' and 'when' as opposed to questions requiring a 'yes' or 'no' answer).

Developing the quality of your listening in this way is likely to make a considerable difference to your learning and to your relationships with people generally. It will make you more open to new ideas and more in tune with what people are really saying.

Being aware of assumptions

All of us have a set of assumptions – certain underlying beliefs, principles, generalisations and notions – that we acquire and carry with us through life. We are often only partially aware that they exist, however, since they have been absorbed only half-consciously and have never been critically examined.

The problem with assumptions is that many of them simply will be untrue and, as a consequence, they will limit our ability to see reality or the full facts of the matter in question. Because we are often unwilling to acknowledge our assumptions to other people, they can remain unchallenged indefinitely.

Our assumptions can also prevent us from listening to others, particularly where they are talking about something which makes us feel uncomfortable or challenges our underlying beliefs.

Open learning can, however, help us to bring our assumptions out into the open as it provides a non-threatening environment in which we can face up to our attitudes. Having done this, we can then go on to evaluate critically what we believe and perhaps re-shape our views as a result of this.

It is important, therefore, to try to become aware of where and how we have acquired our views and attitudes, and in particular to be aware of when we are not approaching our studies with an open mind.

In addition, we need to be mindful that others will have assumptions as well and to take this into account when we are hearing or reading about another's views.

Endnote

This chapter has concentrated on the techniques and methods that you can apply to make your reading and listening as effective as possible. In particular, the importance of being selective in the materials you study has been discussed, and the need to establish a purpose to reading as well as an appropriate approach.

The importance of being active in your reading and listening, searching for meaning behind the written text or spoken word, and thereby gaining a full understanding of the subject matter that is being communicated, has also been examined.

In this chapter we have looked at:

- How you might approach your reading
- The materials that are available to you
- The importance of establishing your purpose before you begin your reading
- How to select your reading
- How to preview a book or article
- The multi-stage approach to reading
- How to develop active listening
- Being aware of assumptions.

6. Taking notes

This chapter explores why we take notes, the different contexts in which notes are taken and methods of recording information in note form. It also looks at some of the problems students can experience when taking notes and whether different learning situations call for different approaches.

The chapter concludes with a brief look at how to review and store your notes when you have completed them.

Why take notes?

Open learning course materials usually have a clear and easily identifiable structure, signposted with main headings and subheadings which you can be confident are complete, accurate and well presented. If you are on one of these courses, you may feel there is less need for you to take notes than is the case for students on a traditional course. However, as we have already seen, there is always a need to supplement and enhance core materials through other sources. It is likely that, whatever course you are on, you will be in learning situations which require you to generate your own notes.

The following are some other reasons for taking notes.

1. To keep a record of your learning sources and the key information or learning points of a particular piece of study.

2. To keep abridged versions of complicated or lengthy information. This may reveal a structure or hierarchy of ideas which may not be readily apparent when reading the original material.

3. To help you to remember key points.

4. To extract meaning from words. The very process of reading to condense material into note form requires you to analyse and critically reflect on what the writer or lecturer is saying. This helps you to formulate your own opinions and put the material into context in relation to your experiences.

5. Notes in your own words may be easier to understand.

6. To highlight areas you don't fully understand. If you are unable to re-phrase or condense something, for example, it may be that you don't understand the concepts involved.

7. To act as revision aids by listing key words or ideas.

8. To help you remain actively involved and attentive.

9. To review a learning session.

10. To test your understanding of your reading, as we saw in the previous chapter.

11. To help you plan your work for an assignment or presentation.

12. To capture good ideas, moments of inspiration, critical incidents, work and life experiences, as well as your own reactions, feelings and thoughts about what you are experiencing. (This may involve keeping a critical diary, as discussed in Chapter 3.)

As you can see, there are a wide variety of reasons for taking notes. It is important to stress, however, that note-taking is a creative process which actively involves you in reacting to the material you are reading, listening to or seeing. This means that your notes are likely to be very different from those of another student as they will reflect your own thoughts, ideas and learning needs.

Problems associated with note-taking

One of the main problems with note-taking is that unless you make a special effort to focus on your own understanding, it is easy for it to become a passive activity. This inevitably results in your failing to structure your notes in line with your own learning goals and can lead you to produce lengthy notes that simply regurgitate what has been written, often in the writer's own words and in such a way that they are no easier to follow or use than the main text itself. The same can apply to note-taking from the spoken word.

Furthermore, unless you have a clear idea about what you want from your notes, the process can be very time-consuming and wasteful as you may be unable to decide what to include and what to leave out. On the other hand, if your goals are very narrow, you might lose information which could prove valuable later on.

Many students find that their notes are not as useful as they would like or that they don't use them nearly as much as they thought they would. The main reasons seem to be:

• The notes are not clear or easily readable
• They lack focus or direction
• It is difficult to distinguish between key and supplementary information (that is, the hierarchy of ideas)
• The notes are incomplete.

Tony Buzan, in his book, *Use Your Head*[1], argues that one of the main reasons students fail to make proper use of their notes is the way they are formulated and presented. He estimates that 90 per cent of our time is wasted in recording and then re-reading unnecessary words, and that the tendency to write notes out in full sentences interferes with the process our brain uses to search for and connect key words or ideas. This is explored below in the section on methods of taking notes.

When to take notes

Some students prefer to take notes only when they are writing essays; others use notes for a wider range of purposes. What works for you will depend on your preferred style of learning, as well as the particular learning goals you have at the time.

Whether or not to take notes

As note-taking can be time-consuming, it is worth considering alternative approaches when they are appropriate. You may, for example, decide to annotate, highlight or underline text in your own materials.

Where there are large sections of relevant information within a particular library book, you may decide to photocopy these and highlight the appropriate information. This is a very quick and easy way of drawing your attention to salient parts while keeping a permanent record of the full text. It can be particularly useful during revision, but you need to be careful that it doesn't become a passive activity and that you continue to interact with what is written.

It is essential to keep checking your understanding as you work through the materials. It is also useful to annotate in the margins any comments or questions that occur to you so that you have a record of your views and reactions to what you are reading. This will help you when you are generating ideas for an essay.

Where you have only temporary access to materials and want to extract certain parts – for example, when preparing for an assignment – it is likely that you will want to take notes. Also, where there is information which you feel might be useful later on, you may view it as a wise investment of your time to take some notes now. The obvious difficulty with this is knowing what may be of use to you in the future, in which case it may be that you decide to note down the details of the publication so that you can return to it later if need be. Index cards are very useful for keeping a record of the full details of texts to which you have referred. Not only is this essential for referencing purposes, but, if you annotate the cards, they are a valuable reminder of where you can find useful material on particular topics.

What to take notes on

The content of your notes will depend very much on your overall objectives, but is likely to include some or all of the following:

- Key elements such as main ideas, theories, opinions, facts, data, characters
- Major stages, steps or processes
- The hierarchy of ideas, that is, how the main ideas fit together
- Material you find of particular interest, that surprises you or that you find especially illuminating or controversial
- The author's aims, assumptions, bias, opinions
- Items you want to follow up
- Your own thoughts, ideas, opinions, reactions
- Cross-references to other sources, links with other materials, comparisons and contrasts
- An overview of a particular piece of work
- Information on the source itself, including author, title, edition and page numbers. This is crucial in case you need to refer to the book again or for acknowledging your sources when you write an essay.

Bear in mind what we have discussed already about most people taking too many notes. Keep your notes brief and use your own words to summarise the points you want to record. Avoid writing notes about things that you can easily look up when you need to.

ACTIVITY 1
Examine a set of notes that you made recently and consider the following questions:

- **How meaningful are those notes to you now?**
- **What purpose do the notes serve in relation to your study plan?**
- **What, if any, learning goals did you have in mind when you prepared the notes?**
- **Do your notes meet these goals?**

If you found that your notes were not particularly useful to you, it may have been because you were not pursuing your learning goals. Whatever your response to Activity 1 was, the next section should be helpful in suggesting a different approach to note-taking.

Some different methods of taking notes

There are many different ways of taking notes and the one you choose will vary according to your subject, the information medium used, your aim and personal preference.

Patterned notes

This method has been pioneered by Tony Buzan and is based on research about how people read and remember.

'When people describe books they have read or places they have been to, they do not start to re-read from memory. They give key concept overviews outlining the main characters, settings and events, adding descriptive detail. Similarly, the single key word or phrase will bring back whole ranges of experience and sensation…'[1]

Buzan argues that the notes we take should be in tune with and mirror the way that our brain remembers things by association. Because of this, notes should not use full sentences as this will obstruct the main messages getting through and, in particular, our ability to see the links and connections between one idea and another. The brain, in his view, is better able to make connections if allowed to move quickly from one idea to another without interference from interconnecting words which have little value or meaning.

Using key words and phrases to write notes is a very different approach to the standard note format used by most students and does have a number of advantages. It forces you, for example, to concentrate on the meaning of what is said or written rather than just copying down words. After all, when you come to expand on the notes, such as when you are writing an assignment, you will have to use your own words.

Taking notes in this format should give you more time to listen or to read actively and to capture the essential messages and meanings than if you were trying to write everything down in full sentences.

Buzan favours a patterned note style rather than the traditional linear format. He argues that the layout of notes should follow the processes of the brain and that conventional methods are restrictive and make it difficult for the reader subsequently to identify key information and connections.

The patterned note style was used at the beginning of this book when you thought about the skills you would need while studying. Look back to Figure 1 on page 11 to remind yourself.

By placing the topic or main idea in the middle of the page and surrounding it with your notes, linked by lines, it is easy to see the pattern, or hierarchy of ideas, that we have stressed as being so important. You can develop this by using colours, symbols or other techniques to draw connections and relationships.

Buzan also recommends that where there are features such as graphs, lists, statistics and so on, you record those on the facing page.

ACTIVITY 2
Make notes of this chapter up to this point using the patterned note style.

There is, of course, no right answer to this Activity as your notes are unique to you. However, Figure 2, which can be found on page 86, gives an example of one response which you may like to compare with your own.

Linear approaches to note-taking tend to force a structure which can interfere with the way your brain generates information. This can be particularly problematic if you are taking notes in preparation for writing an essay. Patterned notes, on the other hand, allow your brain to free-flow ideas in no particular order. The advantages of patterned notes are that they:

• Require a minimum of text
• Reduce the risk of plagiarism
• Allow you to brainstorm all your ideas
• Can be adapted to suit your own style
• Enable you to annotate, add later thoughts and ideas easily
• Show a hierarchy of ideas
• Can help you to remember by giving you a visual pattern
• Are an effective tool for planning essays.

If you haven't tried taking notes in pattern form before, you might find it takes some time to get used to such a different approach. Some students complain that notes are difficult to follow in this format, that they don't show the structure of something sufficiently or that they don't find them easy to interpret when they come to review them. However, it is an extremely useful technique, particularly when you are planning an essay, and many students find that, with practice, they are able to overcome any initial difficulties.

Conventional notes

Conventional notes can vary from a skeletal outline with short phrases and key words to to a full précis of a lecture or particular piece of writing using complete sentences. Where you are taking notes from open learning materials, the interconnections between points are already made for you, so it is a relatively straightforward process.

Most people develop their own style of taking notes which may include abbreviations or a personal version of shorthand. You need to be careful about this if you intend to swap notes with other students. It is also likely that you have developed a particular system for distinguishing between main and secondary information. You may, for example, use indentation, bullet points or a numerical and/or alphabetical system to indicate the beginning of new paragraphs, subsections or minor points. Using a linear format in some circumstances can present problems in that it may be difficult for you to distinguish accurately and easily between major and minor points, particularly as there may be multiple and complex relationships between them.

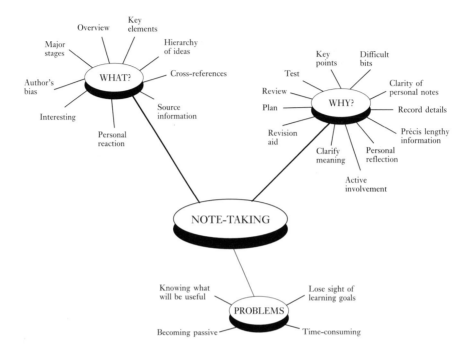

Figure 2. Example of a patterned note style

Making your notes effective
The following are some broad guidelines for effective note-taking:

1. Use a consistent style so you are able to understand your notes easily at a later date. Work out a system for breaking up your material into relevant sections and be consistent in your use of abbreviations.

2. Decide how you are going to distinguish between main and sub-points and, again, be consistent in the methods chosen. You need to use a system which is flexible enough for you to extend it as required and which shows interrelationships and the hierarchical structure of the material. For example, you might have a main section numbered 2, with sub-sections 2.1, 2.2 and so on. Within each sub-section, paragraphs can be further numbered 2.1.1, 2.1.2, etc.

3. Leave wide margins to allow for adding to and annotating your notes.

4. Always include information about the source of your material (title, author, date, publisher, edition, page numbers).

5. Use colour, underlining and capitals to give emphasis where relevant.

6. Write clearly – there is no point in writing everything down if you can't read it later.

Fitting the approach to the situation

Different circumstances are likely to need different approaches. For example, when you are attending a lecture or watching a video or television programme, unless you are able to record what is being said, you will have to make very quick decisions about what to include in your notes and what to leave out. It is a good idea to plan as much as you can beforehand by finding out about the proposed content and formulating your own objectives and questions.

This situation will not occur when you are taking notes from written sources. In these circumstances you are more likely to experience difficulties in knowing how much detail to include and in avoiding straightforward copying of the text. The key to all note-taking is selectivity and recognising what information you already know and what more you need. This is not as easy as it seems. It can be very tempting to carry on taking notes simply for the sake of completeness, especially where the author or lecturer is particularly fluent.

Taking notes from lectures
Writing effective notes during a lecture is a fine balancing act which requires complex listening skills and a concentration on what the lecturer means rather than what he or she says. You need to focus on getting down the notes which give you the information you require, while at the same time actively questioning what is being said and making decisions about what is relevant and what isn't. It can be useful to have an arrangement with one or more fellow students to swap notes. This can help to give you another perspective on the lecture and to check that you have covered all the major points. However, bear in mind that taking fewer notes in the lecture, but following it up afterwards by reviewing and annotating what you have written, is far more effective for your learning than scribbling down as much as possible of what the lecturer says without absorbing the argument, then filing your notes away until some future date when they may well be incomprehensible.

In Chapter 4 we looked at the type of preparation required before attending a lecture and in particular at the importance of reading up on the subject beforehand. This will enable you to formulate your objectives and also reduce the need for you to take copious notes on information that is already available to you.

The lecturer may issue handouts which list the main points of the lecture. This can free you from writing notes so that you can concentrate on recording your reactions and thoughts about what is being covered.

Structuring your note-taking in lectures

Lecturers will often help you follow the structure of their talk and distinguish the main learning points from supplementary material by using regular reviews and signposting. They do this in various ways, for instance by using questions or key headings. Lecturers often give clues which indicate the relative importance of a particular point or issue and tell you when they are about to move on to another area. Some of these clues may seem very obvious, but can easily be missed in the lecture context if you are not looking out for them. Examples might be:

'My first point is . . .'
'Secondly . . .'
'And finally . . .'
'To summarise . . .'
'I want to move on now and . . .'
'An alternative theory is . . .'
'The main point . . .'
'What I want to emphasise . . .'
'In conclusion . . .'.

The beginning and end of a lecture are of particular importance. The introduction will generally tell you what is going to be covered and the overall aim of the session. The conclusion should then summarise the main points of the lecture and is a good opportunity for you to check that you have got down all the main details and structure of the lecture.

Taking notes from books

As we saw in the previous chapter, there are important benefits to be gained by leaving your note-taking until after you have finished your reading.

First, it enables you to check your learning and your understanding of the material. Second, it will help you to avoid copying down unnecessary detail or using the writer's own words. Third, it will encourage you to evaluate what you are studying and formulate your own views and opinions. (See the discussion on the multi-stage approach in Chapter 5.)

Reviewing and storing your notes

It is important that you review your notes as soon as you can to ensure that they contain all the information that you require, are accurate and that you understand them. This process will help you to consolidate your knowledge and will aid your memory retention. When you are generating information to write an essay you are likely to review your notes as a matter of course. When you are taking notes that you may not need for some time, however, this review process is essential if they are to be meaningful.

It is also useful at this stage to cross-reference your notes with other relevant material, to follow up any questions you have about what has been covered, and to add any further thoughts that have since occurred to you about the topic.

You will find it helpful to establish a filing system for your notes so that they can be easily and quickly located and retrieved as required. The most flexible system is a ring-binder so that you can put in pages and take them out easily. It is also a good idea to keep a page at the front to record the contents.

ACTIVITY 3
Either pair up with a fellow student and swap notes you have both taken on a particular subject, or, if you have a self-help group, try this exercise on a group basis. Compare how each person has taken his/her notes, including the layout, the structure, what has been included, left out and so on. Discuss why these differences have occurred and what changes in each person's approach to note-taking might be beneficial.

There are a number of different ways of taking notes and it is important that you are comfortable with what you choose. If, however, you haven't tried other methods, you will not be able to assess their value for you. You are urged, therefore, to explore different methods so that you can be sure you are using the best method for you in each context.

The effectiveness of your notes will ultimately depend on whether you have fully understood the original material. Your note-taking should therefore encourage you to reflect on what is said or written, to enable you to check your understanding and formulate your response to what is being covered.

Endnote

This exploration of note-taking has, it is hoped, given you some new ideas to try out. Perhaps, if your note-taking has not been satisfactory in the past, you can see why that might be the case and practise approaching it in different ways. You should now be more aware of the pitfalls of copying out notes verbatim from texts or attempting to do so from lectures.

In this chapter we have looked at:

- Why we need to take notes
- Some of the problems associated with note-taking
- When it is appropriate to take notes
- What to take notes on
- Some of the different methods of taking notes, especially the patterned note method
- How to tackle note-taking in various circumstances.

REFERENCE
1. Buzan, T. *Use Your Head*. London: BBC Books, 1989.

7. Writing essays

This chapter looks at the purposes and benefits of writing essays and the main stages involved in the process. It examines a number of different approaches to essay-writing as well as how to define what the essay question is really asking. The differences between essays and reports are discussed. We also point out the importance of developing your own writing style.

You will find it helpful to work on your next essay assignment as you read this chapter, so that you can apply what you are learning as it arises. The Activities are designed to take you through the process of preparing to write an essay. This will mean that you are likely to spend more time on this chapter than you have on previous ones, but it should be time well spent.

If you have not yet reached the stage in your studies where you need to write an essay, you may like to read the chapter through for the general information it contains and return to it at a later date when you have an essay to work on.

ACTIVITY 1
Reflect on your past efforts at essay-writing, including any feedback you have received, and make some notes about where you feel your current strengths lie and the areas which require further development. You may have existing learning goals or information, perhaps within your personal profile, which can help you with this.

Now formulate some questions or a set of objectives which you can address as you work through this chapter and write your next essay assignment.

Why write essays?

Students often see essays purely as methods of assessment or as preparations for examinations which are therefore interruptions to normal studies rather than an integral part of them. This attitude fails to appreciate the substantial benefits to be gained from writing essays.

Essay-writing is important for a number of reasons. The most significant of these is the intellectual development that it brings. Writing essays is an opportunity for you to internalise knowledge gained and to organise your own understanding and thinking about a particular issue or topic. It requires you to research and consider an often diverse set of views and perspectives and to present a rational and comprehensive argument. As part of this process you will need to analyse and critically reflect on your reading in order to produce a piece of work that is coherent and cohesive in relation to the question being asked.

Most, if not all, of the skills that are required of you in this process are important life skills. Even if you have not tackled a piece of academic writing for some time, it is likely that you are practising the necessary skills in other areas. For example, you may have to produce reports as part of your professional life; record-keeping often requires you to formulate and draw together your thoughts and conclusions; writing formal letters can also give you some experience in this area.

Writing essays helps you to plan and organise your studies and draw together as a cohesive whole the work you have been carrying out. It is, therefore, a good idea to write as many essays as you can, as they provide you with a focus for your study, help you to learn actively and give you feedback and encouragement on the progress that you are making.

Essays do, however, tend to concentrate on one aspect of your course. This can make it difficult to make links between the main areas of your study. Some students overcome this problem by reading each others' essays. This enables you to cover a much wider range of topics than might otherwise have been possible and also provides a useful opportunity to see other approaches and viewpoints.

There is no doubt that essays are a valuable, and often the principal, means of generating feedback from tutors as to the progress being made. Knowing just how well you are doing can often be difficult to judge accurately on your own, but is essential if you are to develop your skills and expertise.

Feedback has a number of other benefits:

- It can increase your confidence by confirming your strengths and achievements
- It can encourage and support you when you are feeling insecure or in doubt about your abilities. No matter how experienced or competent you are, you are likely to have moments of uncertainty

- It can show you where you need to improve
- It provides contact with a specialist adviser.

Receiving feedback can be difficult at times and it is easy to reject criticism or feel defensive and annoyed by it. However, your purpose is to learn and grow and you will do this only if you listen to critical comments as well as praise.

Your tutors will undoubtedly have your best interests at heart and want you to succeed. However, some will be better at giving constructive feedback than others. You may need to follow up comments that you don't understand or agree with, or request more comprehensive feedback and guidance in certain areas.

The essay-writing process

There are six main stages to writing an essay, namely:

- Choosing your essay
- Defining your essay question
- Researching your material
- Planning your essay
- Writing
- Reviewing.

Each of these stages will be examined in turn.

Choosing your essay

It is likely, especially if you are an open learner, that you have some degree of choice as to the nature and possibly even the number of essays you write. You may, for example, be given a list of suggested topics and asked to select from these. The topic you choose will depend on a range of different factors.

You may decide to select an essay which covers a topic of special interest or relevance to you. It could be an area that is currently very topical or that affects you directly in your professional life. Alternatively, it could be a subject you find particularly challenging, perhaps a topic you haven't fully got to grips with which it would be beneficial for you to research in depth. This would also enable you to consolidate and check your understanding through the essay-writing process and generate some feedback from your tutor. However, you may prefer to play on your strengths, particularly if the essay will form part of your overall assessment. In this case, you would choose something which you find easier and are more confident about. Finally, you may decide to use the essay-writing process to involve you in some new learning, so that you can move your studies forward.

As you can see, there are a number of factors for you to weigh. Your choice is most likely to depend on whether and to what extent the essay constitutes part of your final assessment, as well as how confident you feel about your own abilities. This is entirely understandable, but at the same time it is important that you consider essays as part of your overall personal development and do not always avoid topic areas which are more demanding or challenging.

ACTIVITY 2
Select an essay to tackle as you work through this chapter, or, if you have already chosen one, review your reasons for your choice. What was the basis on which you made your decision? Discuss the reasons for your choice with others – fellow students, colleagues, family. What do they feel about the rationale you have used? Are you still happy with the choice you have made or do you feel you might like to try a different approach, now or next time?

Defining your essay question

This is often the most difficult part of writing essays and the one that examiners and tutors identify as the main cause of loss of marks.

Taking an essay question at face value without careful consideration can result in your missing the point entirely. However accurate, comprehensive, well-written or original the answer, if it fails to address the issues or question contained within the essay title, you will not achieve a pass mark. This is therefore an area that calls for careful planning.

Essay questions are often not that easy to interpret. In general reading, linking words are normally secondary to the main text and so we tend to overlook these when we read. In essay questions, however, the opposite is often true, so it is very easy to miss important clues as to what the essay question is really looking for. An essay asking: 'How does the government see the role of the community midwife...?', for example, requires a very different answer than would be the case if it began with: 'How should the government see the role of the community midwife...?'. It is easy to see in these circumstances how students can find themselves answering the wrong question. Just one word alters the whole slant of the question, transforming it from a relatively straightforward descriptive type of essay to one that is evaluative and analytical.

There are a number of approaches that you can take to help you to define what your essay question is asking. For example, you can:

1. Look up each word in the dictionary
This is often helpful in giving you alternative ways of looking at things, particularly the linking words, so that you can see if there are any subtle differences between your own understanding of a word and the standard version.

2. Brainstorm your ideas
Brainstorming is a very useful problem-solving technique that can be applied in many different situations. The advantage of this type of technique is that it tends to yield a far wider and more original set of ideas than would be possible using our normal thought processes. This is because it encourages both sides of the brain to function. Most of us tend to under-utilise one side of the brain and many of us are conditioned to disregard the more creative side. Brainstorming helps us to see things from a more lateral point of view.

In addition, the technique enables us to shed limitations on the way we think by allowing the brain free rein. Unlike conventional filing systems, the brain stores its information in various pockets and accesses these when an idea in one pocket sparks off an association with another idea held elsewhere. In order to gain full access to these memory and ideas files the brain must be allowed to work without restriction or interruption.

This means that a brainstorming session can leave you with a large amount of irrelevant information, but it also usually brings up ideas that might never have been accessed under normal circumstances. In addition, an idea which at first seems worthless may on closer inspection yield dividends and should not be dismissed without being given some thought.

Some tips for brainstorming:

- Use a large sheet of paper
- Don't stop to analyse or refine your ideas, just write them down
- Write everything down, however ridiculous it may seem
- Don't try to order your ideas or structure them at this stage
- Use the patterned note style which was discussed in Chapter 6. Put the topic in the middle of the page and scatter your ideas around it, using main and sub-branches
- Spend about 10 minutes on this exercise
- Having brainstormed, you can then select and refine those ideas which are of use to you.

3. Rephrase the essay question in your own words
Rewriting the question in your own words can help you to interpret what is required by getting you to express it in a way that makes more sense to you. Essay titles tend to hold a lot of information within a single question, so you might need to write more than one sentence to extract the full meaning.

4. Write down the opposite of the question
This may seem a rather odd thing to do, but it can be helpful in ensuring that you cover all aspects of a question and understand what is relevant and what is not. If we did this in the earlier example, for instance, it might read: 'How shouldn't the government see the role of the community midwife . . . ?'. Brainstorming this question as well as the one asked may raise some additional issues and information which can be incorporated into your answer. It can also help you to provide a well-balanced answer and to encompass a broader perspective.

5. Discuss the meaning of the question with colleagues, friends and fellow students
Asking others for their interpretations or brainstorming can reveal alternative meanings or approaches.

6. Check your assessment of what you think the question means against the general level of the course and follow up any concerns
You will very quickly begin to get a feel for the level of your course and the degree of difficulty or complexity it involves. Where you have identified an essay question as being at a level which surprises you, it is a good idea to check this to make sure you pitch your answer appropriately. This doesn't mean that a descriptive type of question will never be asked at degree level or that an evaluative question won't be posed on a lower-level course. However, as you progress on your course you can expect it to become more demanding in line with your development, and you should therefore act on

any instinct which tells you that you may be mistaken in your interpretation of what is required.

Essay question terminology

There are a number of terms that frequently crop up in essay questions which you need to be sure you fully understand so that you can appreciate the kind of answer that is required. They are listed with their descriptions below.

Analyse: Thoroughly examine something by breaking it down into its constituent parts or stages

Apply: Employ knowledge in a practical or appropriate way

Argue: Present the case for and/or against something

Compare: Show the similarities between things

Contrast: Show the differences between things. Note that while some essays ask you to compare and contrast, others may ask you simply to compare, but there may also be an implicit expectation that you should highlight the main differences. Where you can, seek clarification over this as it is an area where it is easy to misinterpret the extent of what is expected. If this is not possible, you will need to decide what approach to take and make this apparent in your introduction.

Define: Give the exact meaning

Describe: Give a detailed account

Discuss: Examine or argue about something, including reasons for and against

Evaluate: Critically appraise and determine the worth or value of something in the light of facts and evidence. This includes giving your own personal opinion

Examine: Carry out an investigation or study

Explain: Give reasons for something. Interpret or make something clear

Expand: Fill out, add to or develop, for example, an argument or theory

Illustrate: Clarify something through giving examples or by the use of diagrams, graphs, or charts

Interpret: Draw out the meaning or significance. This involves giving your own understanding

Justify:	Show sufficient or valid reasons for something
Outline:	Show the main features, principles and structure of something, omitting minor details
Review:	Look back over and examine something critically
Summarise:	Précis main points or features.

ACTIVITY 3
In the light of what you have read, redefine your chosen essay question and come to some decisions as to what the essay is about and what you will need to include.

When you have done this, compare it with your usual procedure.

Researching your material

This stage should be relatively straightforward provided you have defined your essay question well and know exactly what you are looking for. The processes involved in reading actively (Chapter 5) and taking notes (Chapter 6) are clearly important aspects of researching your material. If you feel you need to, review those topics before moving on.

Formulating a set of questions
Part of the research stage is to formulate a set of questions to help you to remain focused and actively questioning as you work through potential material. It is also likely that additional and more specific questions will begin to emerge as you progress with your research.

One technique that is recommended by many students is that of keeping a notebook beside you at all times. This can be an invaluable study aid as it enables you to capture potentially valuable ideas and information as they occur, many of which would otherwise be lost or forgotten. Some students keep a page for each potential essay question while others simply record information on a subject-by-subject basis. This technique has a further advantage in that it allows your subconscious mind to be used to good effect. As you have probably found when you are faced with a particularly difficult problem or situation, it can often help to stop thinking about it for a few days, after which time a solution may suddenly become apparent. This is because you have given your subconscious mind a chance to work on the problem.

Finally, remember to make a record of your sources in case you need to refer to them again, as well as to enable you to include them in your essay. Any direct copying of text must be placed in quotation marks and the author credited.

ACTIVITY 4
Draw up a set of questions to help you collect the material you require for your essay.

How did this compare with your usual method?

Planning your essay

The next step is to produce a detailed plan of how your essay will be organised. Some students attempt to bypass this stage, viewing it as an unnecessary or additional burden. However, a comprehensive essay plan will undoubtedly save you time later by providing you with a coherent framework and structure within which to organise your materials. Without a plan you will probably need to do several drafts of your essay before producing an answer with which you are fully satisfied.

How much detail you include in your plan is a matter of personal choice. It might be a few words jotted down on a scrap piece of paper or a detailed plan of each paragraph. Provided your own method works well for you, then there is no reason to change. However, some students never consciously make a decision about the best way to plan and tend to take what appears to be the quickest and easiest route. This will not necessarily save you time as, generally, the more detailed and well-thought-out the plan, the more straightforward a task you are setting yourself when you come to write your essay.

Whatever you decide, it is important that you use this stage to review all the notes you have gathered, to discard unnecessary or irrelevant material and to group and order the remainder into a structure that addresses the essay question clearly and effectively.

The next section discusses structure and at the end of it you will be given an Activity in which you plan your essay and take it to the next stage.

Deciding on a structure

Precisely how you organise your material will depend on both the nature of the essay question and also on your own individual style.

You may come across very precise instructions as to the type of layout required; for example, 'List . . .', or 'Write a report . . .', and you are likely to lose marks if you ignore them. Even where the instructions are not so prescriptive, there are usually clues as to the type of approach you should adopt. For example, certain essay titles may call for an analysis of something which occurs over a period of time, such as a life's work, the evolution of a particular philosophy or way of thinking, or the origin and development of a particular field of research. Where this is the case you may decide to order your material chronologically. But first you need to consider certain factors before deciding whether this is the most suitable or straightforward approach.

With an analytical type of essay there are often many different issues to be addressed and some or all of these may have occurred at separate times. You may have difficulty fitting your material into a rigid chronological framework while retaining its integrity and natural flow.

Suppose, for example, you have been asked to prepare an essay on the evolution and development of public health care. Your answer would need to address, among other things, social, economic and political factors. Using a single chronological order could result in a very disjointed answer as you would need to jump from social to political issues, and so on. This would also give you little opportunity for the analysis of interrelationships, particularly between events occurring at different times. Furthermore, when addressing this sort of essay question, it is likely that some of the factors involved take on a particular prominence at different periods of time. Knowing at what point in time to begin and when to stop can also be difficult.

Chronologically-organised essays are therefore not quite as easy to control as might first appear. It is very easy to get bogged down in detail and end up with an extremely lengthy factual essay which fails to address the main issues or analyse the question in any real depth. The structure can be unwieldy and lack the clarity and conciseness of other approaches. In almost every case it is better to have a structure which is less rigid and which you can control and adapt as necessary.

An alternative approach is to divide your material into relevant groupings or sub-topics. Taking again the example above of an essay on the evolution and development of public health care, there could be separate sections for social factors, economic factors and so on. Alternatively, you might prefer to retain a chronological sense to your essay and divide it into periods of time, such as early, mid and late 19th century. This is a far more flexible structure as it allows you to show developments through time as well as to focus on particular issues. In addition, it shows that you have clearly mastered your subject as you have to be able to analyse your material in order to regroup it yourself.

Grouping material like this tends to result in an essay which looks better organised, provided you use regular signposting such as headings, subheadings and summaries or reviews. It also allows you to get to the heart of the issues more quickly, thereby avoiding the inclusion of material that is irrelevant or too basic. However, you do need to ensure that your groupings do not result in your repeating material, perhaps because they overlap too much.

There are a number of other ways in which you can group your material. You may decide to group together information which has some kind of causal effect on the issue under discussion. If this approach was used for your essay on the development of public health care, for example, you might have a section on the industrial revolution and the growth of the philanthropic movement. Alternatively, if your essay offers you the opportunity to present your answer in the form of an objective and logical argument, you may decide to group your material in a way that highlights the strengths, weaknesses and differences between a number of different viewpoints.

Where there isn't a logical order within the material itself you still need to consider the overall structure of your essay to ensure that it flows logically and is easily understood. In these circumstances you may decide to place your points in order of importance.

Whatever structure you choose, it needs to be logical, easily understood and have a clear beginning, middle and end. It is also a good idea to include an explanation of the structure in the introduction.

Pitching your answer at the right level
The importance of pitching your essay at an appropriate level was mentioned earlier. Understanding the level of knowledge required for your course will enable you to make informed decisions about what to include and at what level.

If you include too much information, particularly of a basic nature, you are in danger of producing an over-long answer which is pitched at too low a level. On the other hand, you don't want to neglect key features or oversimplify things in an attempt to keep your essay concise. Knowing where to pitch your work will become easier as you progress with your course. In addition, the following activities will help:

- Discussing your intended approach and proposed content with colleagues and fellow/former students
- Chatting it over with your tutor
- Looking at past essay questions and model answers
- Looking through work completed by previous students (your tutor or library may have some past papers)
- Picking up clues within the core materials or in any guidance or recommendations issued
- Forming a writing group (this is discussed later in this chapter).

Levels of essay-writing

You will probably find that what is required will fit into one of the following categories:

1. A knowledge of facts

This is a very basic level that enables you to tell others what you know about, for example, events which took place, definitions, theories, research, classifications and principles. If you were writing about reflective practice within the nursing profession, you might state the techniques involved.

2. Interpretation

At this level you would have to demonstrate an understanding of the facts involved. Using again the example of reflective practice, you would need to provide an explanation of the techniques involved in reflective practice rather than a straightforward statement of facts.

3. Application of learning

This is a higher level still, and asks you to apply what you know to real situations. For example, you would be expected to carry out a critical reflection on incidents provided within the essay question or volunteered by yourself.

4. Analysis of learning

This is an even higher level which asks you to break up the knowledge you have into its constituent elements. In writing about critical reflection, for example, you would need to compare this technique with other methods of reviewing performance and to come to some conclusions about its strengths, weaknesses, uses, and benefits.

5. Synthesis of knowledge

This is a still higher level, which is reflected in the ability to bring together different elements of what you know and present them in a new way, or to put forward a new idea. In our example, therefore, you might develop new ideas for reflecting on your experiences or propose policies for the implementation of reflective practice in other sectors or areas of medicine.

As already seen, a course or even a single essay may require you to operate at different levels. Learning to operate at a higher level, perhaps for a degree course, is a gradual process. Many courses increase in complexity in order to reflect an anticipated level of intellectual growth and development in the student.

Knowing the level of learning that is expected of you will not only help with pitching your essay at the right level, but should inform your studies generally.

Planning your introduction and conclusion

Your introduction provides an outline of what you are going to say and needs to include:

1. Your essay definition

This states how you have interpreted the question and the range or limits of your answer. This is particularly important if the range of your topic is very wide. You may need to justify why you have decided to focus on specific aspects at this point.

2. Your structure

This will include the approach you have taken, and why.

3. Definitions of terms central to your essay

Only if necessary.

At this point you may want to include other specific information such as the particular argument you will be putting forward or to use a quote which sums up the central issues. The important thing is to keep your introduction brief and concise to enable you to move on to the main body of the essay as quickly as possible. As a very rough guide, if you find that your introduction is taking up more than three-quarters of a page, you may need to think about condensing it. Some students write their introduction only when they have finished writing the essay itself, which can help to avoid the pitfalls. In this case the second paragraph of your essay may turn out to be a good introductory paragraph.

The traditional essay structure is in three parts:

- Tell them what you are going to tell them
- Tell them
- Tell them what you have told them.

While it is not necessary to be tied to this, the introduction certainly should establish the background of the essay, and the conclusion should summarise the main ideas and points of your argument. You may want to relate the conclusion back to what you said in your introduction, but, most importantly, keep it brief.

One final point about both the introduction and conclusion: be careful that you don't make any false statements about what is in your essay.

Following your conclusion, you need to include a bibliography and references. These will be discussed later in this chapter in the section on report-writing.

You might like to review this section on planning an essay before doing Activity 5.

ACTIVITY 5
Take some time to plan your essay. Make sure that you review your material and decide your line of argument.

Decide on a structure that will be the most effective and plan the points you want to make.

Consider the level of learning that you feel you need to be working to and, if you are uncertain, discuss it with your tutor or a fellow student.

Writing

Developing an appropriate writing style, as was discussed in Chapter 1, is an area which tends to concern students. However, if you have a firm grasp of your material and an organised plan to work to, you should have little trouble writing clearly, simply and concisely. While accepting that there are certain rules in academic writing, such as the need for references and bibliographies, the overall goal is the same as that of any other form of writing. You are aiming to communicate what you want to say to someone else in a way that can be understood easily. For this reason you need to avoid anything that blocks this process, such as unnecessary padding or the use of jargon which is only likely to obscure what you are trying to say and irritate the reader.

Writing effectively therefore involves the following:

1. Thinking through each paragraph so that one flows on from another. It is a good guideline to think of each paragraph as containing one main point; this could be a completely new point or one that is developing a theme. It is also good practice to use the first sentence as a topic sentence which explains what the rest of the paragraph is about.

2. Using simple and concise language. Avoid long, rambling sentences, waffle, padding, unnecessary jargon and long words. Keep to short paragraphs and short sentences.

3. Continually reminding yourself of what you want to say, and why.

4. Thinking about your readers and what they need to be told.

5. Responding to new thoughts and directions as you write. The very process of writing will often stimulate new ideas which you will want to capture. Do not stifle good ideas just because they were not in your original essay plan; this may mean that you need to revise your plan to incorporate them.

6. Accepting that there are times when words will flow more easily than others. This is only natural and there are techniques to help you when you are experiencing difficulties (which we will explore next).

7. Acknowledging the value of your own thoughts and opinions, although you always need to distinguish clearly between your own ideas and those of others.

Wherever possible, use a word processor as this will save you time re-writing; your first attempt will certainly need revision. Using double-spacing and wide margins gives the essay a clear and uncluttered appearance, especially if you have made some insertions after printing or writing it. It is also advisable to use one side of the page only.

When writing is difficult

At times you might find yourself suffering from what is commonly known as 'writer's block', when the words just won't come and ideas seem jumbled or confused.

A useful technique for overcoming this is 'free writing'. This is not dissimilar to the brainstorming technique discussed earlier. It involves writing without concerning yourself about whether it is good enough, whether it follows your plan or whether the spelling or grammar is correct. Don't attempt to amend what you are writing and don't stop, even if you think you are writing rubbish; simply write down whatever comes into your head. Once the ideas begin to flow again you can either continue as you are or go back and edit what you have written before returning to your plan. You will probably be surprised to find that much of what you have written is useful. This technique can also help you to formulate your own writing style. You may even decide to use it to write the first draft of your essay.

Although the 'free writing' technique will work in many cases, there may be other times when it is sensible to leave writing altogether for the moment and come back to it later.

Developing your own writing voice

All of us, even though we might not recognise it, have a writing style of our own. The first step in the process of developing your own writing voice is to recognise your experience of writing and the approach that you have tended to take in the past. This is not only in relation to academic writing. You might, for example, be a keen letter writer or enjoy writing poetry or prose. You might have to produce business reports or letters for work or for a voluntary organisation or club. You may be keeping or have kept a diary. If you are developing a profile you will almost certainly be getting practice and developing skills in writing.

One of the most effective ways of improving your technique is to write regularly and as much as possible. You don't need a reason for writing and if you practise using a variety of different forms it will help you in developing a more formal style.

You might like to try experimenting with some writing of your own – whether 'creative' or practical – and perhaps sharing it with friends or forming a writing group with fellow students. You would then receive feedback from people who share similar aspirations and concerns and gain experience of a wider variety of styles and techniques.

Reviewing

Leaving your essay for a few days will enable you to approach it with a fresh eye and see things that would not have been apparent had you reviewed it immediately on completion, when you are still too close to the material to see it clearly and objectively.

Do not expect to complete your essay review at one reading. It is very difficult to hold in mind more than one perspective at once. Reading to check grammar and spelling, for example, requires a completely different approach from that required to read for content or clarity of style. You will need to read through your essay several times, concentrating on a different aspect each time.

It is a good idea to use a checklist to ensure that you have included everything you need to. You might like to develop your own, but you can use the checklist given below as a guide.

Essay review checklist

Content
- Have I answered the question?
- Is all the material included relevant?
- Is it at all repetitive?
- Is it pitched at the right academic level?
- Have I included my own ideas?
- Are my ideas supported by facts or evidence?
- Have I presented an objective, well-balanced argument?

Structure
- Is there a flow to my argument?
- Have I explained the structure and is it easily understandable and clear?
- Are there clear signposts?
- Do my introduction and conclusion relate to the main body of the essay?
- Have I included accurate references and a bibliography?

Style
- Is the language clear, simple and concise?
- Does every sentence say what I want it to?
- Have I used an appropriate format?
- Are there any very long sentences or paragraphs that need to be condensed or broken up?

Presentation
- Have I checked thoroughly for any spelling mistakes or grammatical errors?
- Does the essay look polished?

Asking a friend, colleague or another student to comment on your finished essay is very useful in the reviewing process. If you set up a writing group, this could become a regular agenda item.

Writing reports

You may be asked to produce a report, rather than an essay, during your studies if you are conducting a piece of research or carrying out an investigation. The results of your detailed analysis will be presented in a report which will include your major findings and deductions and any proposals or recommendations for future action. Report-writing is a valuable life skill which is worthwhile developing if you have the opportunity.

The conventions used in reports such as scientific research papers are beyond the scope of this book, as is the nature of a lengthy piece of investigative research. However, we will look at the layout of reports, as this follows a fairly standard pattern. Bear in mind that the main focus of any report you write as part of your studies will be the content and nature of the work you have carried out. Good presentation can never disguise poor content.

The purpose of reports

Reports are produced to provide busy readers with the opportunity to digest the main or key findings of substantial research without having to get bogged down in minutiae or specifics. They therefore require the writer to:

- Understand the key points and distinguish between their own agenda and views as to what is significant and those of their readers
- Communicate these key points clearly, concisely and simply
- Present the material in a way that is interesting to readers and stimulates them to read on
- Focus the report precisely in relation to the needs and perspectives of the readers.

Although one can argue that all of these skills are necessary when writing a good essay, they take on an added dimension when writing a report.

The sections of a report

Unlike an essay, a report is broken up into specific sections geared to presenting particular information. These are identified as follows.

Title page

This should describe the subject of the report, the writer's name, the date, the course, and, if appropriate, the name of the company for whom it has been written.

Abstract (also called summary or synopsis)

This is usually a single paragraph which gives a précis of the report, including its aims, findings and conclusions. Its purpose is to give an idea of the contents so that the reader can decide whether to read the report in full. Although this occurs at the beginning, you will not be able to write it until the report has been completed.

Contents page

This enables the reader to see the structure of the report and where to find particular sections.

Introduction

This gives the background to the report and includes most of the features one would expect to find in a normal essay. It may also include whatever background information is deemed necessary to acquaint the reader with the present situation, as well as the methodology used when carrying out the research, for example, the size of the sample and the methods used, such as questionnaires, interviews or literature searches.

Some reports may have a separate section on methodology if this is particularly important or involved (such as in a scientific study).

Findings

This is the main body of the report. It can often become very bulky and you may decide, for the sake of clarity, to include only main points of interest and to attach the rest as appendices at the end of the report. Dividing the material into sections will also help in its presentation.

Conclusions

These should be your main deductions from the findings, substantiated and cross-referenced to relevant evidence, facts or theories.

Recommendations

These can be suggestions for future action or for taking a particular philosophical view or approach. For example, you might recommend a different way of looking at or thinking about something. Whatever you recommend needs to be backed up by the findings put forward in the main body of your report.

Appendices

These should contain any additional information not presented in your report. They still need to be relevant to your main aims and should be referred to in the appropriate parts of the report.

Bibliography and references

A bibliography is a complete list of the sources that you consulted during the preparation of your report or essay. A reference list should give full details of all the references cited within the report and normally precedes the bibliography. References are important as they give the sources of the material you have mentioned, paraphrased or quoted in your main text. As with your bibliography, they show the extent to which you have researched your subject and ensure that you do not take credit for other people's work.

The Further Reading list following this chapter shows how references are laid out. In the case of a book, the author's surname and initials come first, followed by the title of the book in italics (or underlined), then the place of publication, the publisher and the year of publication. For a journal article, the author's surname and initials also come first, followed by the title of the article, the name of the journal (in italics or underlined), the year, volume number, issue number and page numbers.

The bibliography should be in alphabetical order by author's surname. Sometimes the references are listed in the same way, but in reports they are more often listed in the order in which they appear in the text and numbered accordingly. In the text, the appropriate superscript number is given when you refer to that particular book or article.

Alternatively, references can be included within the main text itself (if you want your reader to continue reading uninterruptedly and they are brief) or as footnotes (sometimes accompanied by some comment).

ACTIVITY 6
You should now be in a position to write your essay.

When you have written it, compare it with a previous piece of writing and reflect on what you have learned and any improvements you have noticed.

Now review your learning goals and amend these to reflect your achievements as well as any development needs you have identified.

Endnote

Essay-writing is a skill which, if practised, will contribute substantially to your creative and intellectual development.

Take time to review this chapter and to evaluate the learning that you have achieved. As with everything, it is only by reflecting on both your strengths and weaknesses that you will be able to make informed decisions about what needs to be changed and how this can be done most successfully.

In this chapter we have looked at:

*   The benefits of writing essays
*   The process of planning and writing an essay
*   Writing reports.

Conclusion

This book has covered a wide range of the skills you will need to exploit in order to make the most of your studies. It is to be hoped that you have learnt from it and gained some useful insights into your learning processes and needs, as well as techniques and approaches that will be valuable in your studies and life generally.

Further reading

Boud, D., Keogh, R., Walker, D. *Reflection: Turning experience into learning*. London: Kogan Page, 1985.

Buzan, T. *Make the Most of Your Mind*. London: Pan, 1988.

Buzan, T. *Use your Head*. London: BBC Books, 1989.

Critten, P. *Developing Your Professional Portfolio*. Edinburgh: Churchill Livingstone, 1995.

Davis, M. *A Student's Guide to Open Learning*. London: Macmillan, 1993.

Dunleavey, P. *Studying for a Degree in the Humanities and Social Sciences*. London: Macmillan, 1986.

Freeman, R. *Mastering Study Skills*. London: Macmillan, 1982.

Honey, P., Mumford, A. *The Manual of Learning Styles* (3rd edn). Maidenhead, Berkshire: Honey, 1992.

Honey, P., Mumford, A. *Using Your Learning Styles*. (2nd edn). Maidenhead, Berkshire: Honey, 1995.

Johns, C. The value of reflective practice for nursing. *Journal of Clinical Nursing* 1995; **4**: 23–40.

Kolb, D. *Experiential Learning*. Hemel Hempstead: Prentice Hall, 1983.

Northege, A. *The Good Study Guide*. Buckingham: Open University Press, 1990.

Palmer, A., Burns, S., Bulman, C. *Reflective Practice in Nursing. The growth of the professional practitioner*. Oxford: Blackwell Scientific, 1994.

Robinson, K. M. *Open and Distance Learning for Nurses*. London: Longman, 1989.

Rowntree, D. *Learn How to Study: A practical guide for students of all ages*. London: Macdonald, 1988.

WEEKLY STUDY PLANNER

Time	Mon	Tues	Weds	Thurs	Fri	Sat	Sun
7–8							
8–9							
9–10							
10–11							
11–12							
12–1							
1–2							
2–3							
3–4							
4-5							
5–6							
6–7							
7–8							
8–9							
9–10							
10–11							
11–12							

MONTHLY STUDY PLANNER

Mon	Tues	Weds	Thurs	Fri	Sat	Sun

YEARLY STUDY PLANNER

	Jan	Feb	Mar	Apr	May	June	July	Aug	Sept	Oct	Nov	Dec
Week 1												
Week 2												
Week 3												
Week 4												
Week 5												